This true story tells a journey of discovery and love between a hard-core cat phobic and a stubborn cat.

Kuen-Shan had an innate fear of cats. Her fear was intensified tenfold when a cat insisted on adopting her. This happened shortly after she and her husband moved from London to Wales. A stubborn cat descended from Heaven to invade her personal space at a time when she felt alone, isolated and unhappy.

Healey was a Welsh farm cat. When his owner, Kuen Shan's neighbour, moved away, Healey returned four times to the Welsh hillside where he was born and bred.

Healey turned out to be a Chinese sage in disguise.

By the same author

The Cat and The Tao
The Philosopher Cat
Happy In My Shell

www.kwongkuenshan.net

The Cat Who Loved Me
-and Made Me Love Him

by

Kwong Kuen-Shan

鄺
娟
珊

Kwong Kuen-Shan

- and Made Me Love Him

First published on Create Space 2012

ISBN-13: 978-1477610831

ISBN-10: 1477610839

Cover Design and Illustrations
by
Kwong Kuen-Shan © 2012

For my husband Christopher,

for Healey who shared his destiny with us,
and for Joseph who still purrs for Wales.

Life has an end,
Love has no end.

(Chinese proverb)

- and Made Me Love Him

Introduction: My Cats, My Inspiration

I've learned a few things about cats after years of sharing my home with three of them, and meeting many more. As I watch and wait and watch again, I discover that behind their inscrutable façade cats are intelligent, witty and fun loving. They have immense ingenuity at problem solving and survival. They often outwit humans to get what they want. They also outwit each other to gain superiority in the home or the wild.

I watch again, this time to look beyond the whiskers and discover more; cats seem to have the personality and character traits which were much admired by sages and scholars of ancient China.

My cats have stirred my Chinese mind and brought alive numerous old Chinese proverbs and wise sayings, knowledge that I got from classical Chinese literature and philosophy I studied at school in Hong Kong. Familiar and much loved words unfold before my eyes; words which make me smile a little, cry a little, reflect and contemplate a lot. Many of these words are engraved in my mind so deeply that they can't be erased by decades of living in a non-Chinese culture. I remain an old fashioned, traditional Chinese and I believe in the proverbs and the wise words of my learned ancestors.

I still read these classics, and with every passing year the significance of the thoughts and teaching of the masters makes more sense. I often look at contemporary life through their sayings, many of which I know by heart. This habit means I also see my cats through the masters' teachings.

My cats show me a new perspective. I have become interested in making comparisons between a cat's behaviour and old Chinese thoughts and saying. I look into their behaviour and try to make connections between my observations of them and my Chinese mind. What started as a light distraction from my painting routine turned into an idea for this book.

Contrary to common belief, Chinese sayings are not didactic, severe or outdated, and many are full of wit, wisdom and common sense. The ideas of our wise ancestors are applicable to all humans, in all situations. I've noticed that they don't stop with humans, they apply to cats too.

In my previous books, *The Cat and The Tao* and *The Philosopher Cat,* I related cats to Chinese sayings at an intellectual level. Now, with better insight, I can write about cats with personal feelings, about my own interactions with them, and about how the Classical Chinese wisdom applies to them.

The sayings I have chosen for this book are representative of traditional Chinese thinking and moral conduct. I try to introduce them in a fun and entertaining way. If I succeed in provoking thoughts in my readers, that is a bonus.

We hear stories of men outwitting men, here are stories of cats outwitting cats, cats outwitting humans. We hear stories of love between doting humans and their pets, here is a story of the love between a confirmed cat phobic and a stubborn cat; me and a cat called Healey.

I hope you enjoy our story.

Kwong Kuen-Shan 2012

www.kwongkuenshan.net

1. Cat Dog Man.

Every person attracts praises and criticisms,
Every creature invites love or hatred, likes or dislikes, seldom
indifference.

(Chinese proverb)

I did not dislike cats, detest them, loathe or hate them. The truth was I was terrified of them. I feared everything about them; their dark looks and devil eyes; their hisses and growls and, above all, their menacing teeth and killer claws. They represented everything that was devious and ghostly.

Cats were, in my view, the dark villains and psychotic loners of the animal world. I spent my childhood and most of my adult life avoiding the beasts.

It was all very irrational, as I'd never had a cat, and had no bad experiences with them. I was not unique: some people have phobias for creatures that pose absolutely no danger to them, like bats, mice or spiders. But I wasn't ashamed of my phobia. In fact I made it very clear to any cat lovers kind enough to invite me into their homes that I was petrified of the beasts. Some friends thought I was a bit handicapped, but most tried to treat my fear with sensitivity.

The sensitive friends would shut their cats in a different room, which was OK, if not for the fact that as soon as they heard the slightest scratch, the faintest meow, they let them out! I would of course have pretended not to hear them, even though these noises sent shivers through me. But no, the "little darlings" must not suffer. Out they came!

"I don't believe you," friends would say, "don't be so silly, what can the poor darling do to you!" Meanwhile, the poor darling was forcing its way onto my lap, oblivious to my jumps or screams. Maybe you can fake jumping and screaming, but you can't fake the sweating palms, the pounding heart beat, or the urge to run.

Down to earth friends would take steps to boost my resistance. They would ply me with wine and food, to paralyse me and to render me defenceless. When visiting these houses I took precautions: thick trousers, jumpers, gloves. I even thought about a balaclava. Well, it seemed sensible to me!

Then there were the psychologists. When they found out that I was a confirmed cat phobic, they wanted to know if I had been traumatised while in my mother's womb ("not in my mother's womb, nor anyone else's!", I would answer). "Tell me more about your relationship with your father," one asked, looking deep into my eyes. "My father wasn't a cat!" I replied.

I must admit that my mother was partly credited for my phobia. She hated cats. Ever the good daughter I learned even before I was born that cats were evil and filthy. "Cats smell, cats scratch, cats pee and poo everywhere. Cats have no place in the homes of civilised people," my mother informed me through her abdomen, every day of the 9 months I was in there.

While they might deal with my fears in different ways, these people had one thing in common: they all loved cats. They saw cats as comedians and athletes rolled into one beautiful, flexible body, so they told me. They believed cats are God's best gift to mankind. They believed I was missing out on one of life's great pleasures: the company of a cat.

I certainly didn't see what they loved and they certainly didn't understand my fear.

There are cures for different physical and mental problems;
Except for the incurable ones.

(Chinese proverb)

I believed my phobia was incurable.

****

Years later and nine thousand miles away from my native Hong Kong I met and married Christopher. I didn't marry him for a British passport, which he knew as he had seen my passport before he proposed. I didn't marry him for his money: when we met he had already decided to take time off from medicine to read law. He qualified as a barrister two years later, and was a poor student in the first two years of our married life. No one could call me a gold digger either.

Chris likes cats, he likes cats very much and cats like him very much.

He will stop and talk to any cat he meets when we are out walking. It will acknowledge his greeting by rubbing its head against his legs and purring. When we visit households with cats, within minutes of our arrival the cats will rush forward to greet him with their tails held high like flags. They scramble to sit on his lap. They all want to make his acquaintance. The ones that fail to secure an inch of his lap would sit somewhere opposite him; so that they can look at this magnificent person who understands them. One pretty cat called Jemima invited him to live in HER house so that they could watch television together all the time.

Chris never babies them or sweet-talks to them. He treats them cordially, the same way he would treat someone who offers to buy him a drink in the pub.

"I treat cats as equals, and sometimes they return the compliment," Chris often says.

"They warm to you immediately, and yet they appear to be hostile towards me," I said.

"Try to return the hostility with kindness," Chris replied.

"What do cats know about kindness!"

"You will be surprised; cats know a lot about kindness."

Chris is temperamentally suited to cats. I suspect my husband must have been a cat in his former life.

I found his affinity for cats a little worrying at the beginning. Would he want to keep a cat, or worse, a couple of fluffy kittens? Of course I could retaliate by demanding to have a dog, the bigger and more ferocious the better. I understand dogs. I had an extremely affectionate dog when I was a child. Dogs are uncomplicated. I recognise and respond to their joy and disappointment. I am comfortable in their company. Dogs and humans are made to understand each other, to need each other, to say shamelessly and openly that they love and adore each other. I am emotionally suited to dogs. I believe that the soul of cats is too primitive to understand these emotions.

Chris dislikes dogs. I am baffled; how can anyone dislike man's (and woman's) best friend? (You do or you don't, says Chris). I am more baffled, how can my husband, this six feet and multiple stones man, takes to a dwarf that stands no more than one foot six inches above ground, weighing no more than eight pounds, whiskers included. These dwarfs are equipped with killer claws and teeth which they are just too happy to use. Would we fight over the issue of pets, I wondered. But common sense prevailed; we agree to differ on this subject.

He knew I was frightened of cats. He never pushed for us to have a cat. Being a doctor he knew my phobia, although irrational, was very real. An enthusiastic friend suggested that he should just bring home a couple of kittens.

"THEY will sort her out," she said to him. He told her it wouldn't work because I would sort HIM out. This man who understands cats also understands his woman.

2. The Cat that Eats Last.

After many years living in London we decided to move to Wales. We chose Wales because most of Chris's family live there, and we had been on holiday there a couple of times and liked the place. Also, Chris has always wanted to learn more about wine making. His interest in wine goes beyond the mere consumption of the product. He is interested in the total body of knowledge and the practical application of wine making; from putting grafted cuttings in the ground to bottling and eventually tasting it. He wanted to buy a plot of land in the country where he could cultivate a domestic vineyard. The choice of destination was facilitated by the offer of a job for Chris.

A study of Anglo-Chinese relations demonstrates that the Chinese and the British people know each other well through numerous historic events. The most significant event was in 1842 when China lost the Opium War and the fragrant harbour, Hong Kong was ceded to Britain. The special relationship between Hong Kong and Wales has nothing to do with opium. It is all about the Hong Kong Sevens international rugby tournament, a perennial favourite and an important fixture in the sporting calendar, a festival of rugby's smaller game, held every March in Hong Kong. Rugby is the national religion of Wales (so I am told), and while I am not too interested in rugby, I am proud to point out this association between Wales and Hong Kong.

Wales has a lot in common with my native Hong Kong. They both have hilly landscapes. The hills in Hong Kong are inhabited by millions of people living in sky-scrapers. I have a name for these crowded hills: concrete forests. The hills in Wales are inhabited by thousands of sheep, I also have a name for them: God's paradise. Both peoples respect dragons. Chinese dragons come in a mixture of colours; imperial gold, lacquer red, acid green and indigo. Welsh dragons are red.

One common fact is that not one living Chinese or Welsh person has ever set eyes on a real dragon.

Last but not least the people in both places speak and write an incomprehensible language, which is totally alien to the outside world, and are proud of it. I would feel very at home in Wales, although I had no idea what I would do there.

****

Chris had wanted to buy a house with a 20 miles exclusion zone all round.

"We can live the life of the Chinese sages you aspire to; drink wine in our own bamboo grove and invite the moon to join us." Chris was keen to live in complete isolation.

"Yes, you make all the decision and I'll follow you to the end of the world and the edge of the sky."

This would have been my mother's reply to my father if he had wanted to live in isolation.

"No, these sages were old men who'd had enough of life in the real world. Our combined age is not 100 years yet and I have not had enough of life."

This was my reply.

Married life with a doctor can be lonely, worse if your man is a workaholic who is programmed to (and is young enough) work 24/7, and is happy spending his free time doing other medical related tasks. I knew the score, and I wanted to live in a house with a few neighbours, I would need people around me.

We bought a house on a hillside with a few acres of land which is south east facing, ideal for growing vines. It was a pretty hamlet with only two other houses. Our neighbour in the old farmhouse, Peter and Jo, had three cats, a mother and her two one year old neutered toms. They were black and white farm cats. The two toms were born in the stable next to our garden.

The cats occasionally hunted in our field, but on the whole our paths seldom crossed. The younger of the two toms was called Healey, named after Dennis Healey, a politician who was famous, among other things, for his very thick eyebrows. Jo told me that Healey as a kitten had very bushy whiskers above his eyes. "He and Dennis Healey looked very alike," she said.

I knew a cat called Samurai, one called Mango, and a dog called Asbo.

"I have never heard of any pet called Healey," I said.

"Now you have," Jo said proudly.

"What a peculiar name? Why not Dennis? It is more a cat's name," I thought.

"Healey is simple and dim, non-executive material. No one will ever notice him," Jo concluded.

She fed the cats once a day in the courtyard. She emptied a small tin of cat food into a bowl and left the cats to it. I could see them from my studio window when they fed. The pecking order was that Healey always ate last. He waited by the side as his family gulped down the food. He would gaze ahead as if he had an important decision to make. When his mother and brother finished eating they would move to a sunny spot to wash. Healey would then eat whatever, if any, was left in the bowl. He ate standing up, as if to be ready for a quick get-away.

I knew why Healey didn't eat at the same time as the other two cats; the food bowl wasn't big enough for three heads and he knew it. If he joined in, one of these days the three heads would jam together and it would be very embarrassing for the whole cat family and their owners. Healey didn't want that embarrassment.

I noticed Healey. I unconsciously got into the routine of stopping for a cup of tea at the time when the cats were fed, just to see Healey. I would will him to push his family aside from the food and eat FIRST, and sitting down. He never did.

"Why is he the fattest and the biggest of the three?" I asked Chris.

"He has a corner shop in the field, where he gets fresh rabbits and mice," Chris said. "I often see him hunt, he jumps and kills like a tiger. Healey is no dim wit, he is a world class hunter."

One of the Chinese classics had Healey's number, all right:

Hide your talents behind dim-wittedness:
Do not display your cleverness too readily.
Conceal your clarity behind muddiness,
Step back a little before making an advance.
These are tactics for self-preservation,
These are ways to avoid life's dangers.

(Hung Ying-ming 1573 – 1620)

(Scholar and philosopher)

My mother said to me the night before I left Hong Kong for London, "For the first time in your life you'll be on your own in a foreign land; act dim, hide your cleverness, do not compete with or show off to people who are not worth it."

At the time it sounded almost laughable. I was young; everything was clear to me and everything was achievable. I was not afraid to show off; I wanted the world to take notice of me. Years later, and wiser, I saw and learned to appreciate the significance of my mother's parting words.

Sadly my mother is no longer with us. The youngest daughter of a big family, she was not given the benefit of education. She often made me laugh with her sage remarks on life. On reflection they all made great sense. My mother was the plainest and the most ordinary looking person this planet has ever seen. But so often is the case with wise but modest people, what you see is not what you get. She didn't make any waves in her life, but her fortitude and common sense has made her a major force in mine.

Did Healey know something that my mother had known all those years ago? How could he? A cat's primitive brain could never achieve that level of reasoning.

Healey was the most ordinary looking cat that the Great One had ever created. In the days to come he would demonstrate that he was no ordinary moggy: he was in a class of his own. What you saw was not what you got.

Do not judge people by their appearances,
Judge them by their deeds.

(Chinese proverb)

3. A Cat's Return.

There is no river that cannot be crossed,
No mountain that cannot be conquered.

(Chinese proverb)

A year after our arrival at the hamlet Peter and Jo moved away. They took all their pets with them; horses, dogs, sheep, goats, and the three cats. Two weeks later, a black and white cat staggered into the old farmhouse kitchen, dirty and looking for food. He got the shock of his life to see two large dogs. In a flash, they were on to him, and nearly caught him. He just made it up the grass bank, a split second ahead of them, so our new neighbours in the farmhouse told us.

It was Healey, of course. He had returned, and, thinking he was home, headed for the Aga. No go, under new management! After a few attempts he gave up, and started hunting in our field. We had no dogs, the only house of the three, so our land became Healey's hunting ground.

He didn't stay long. We phoned Peter, and he came to take him back. Healey had disappeared on the first night in their new home, after staring grumpily at the door all afternoon. He walked back 5 miles. On the way there was a dual carriageway, roundabouts, a wide river, and a canal (how did he cross those? Bridges?!). He also climbed 500 feet up the hillside. It took him two weeks.

One week later, I saw him in our field again. "That cat is back!" I screamed, hoping the noise would frighten him off. No luck. We contacted Peter again. He came to fetch him. "We will lock him up this time!" he said, as he drove away with Healey crouched grumpily on the back seat.

Three weeks later he was back. "I will chain him to the stable door!" his exasperated owner told us when he drove him away. A simple deduction revealed that it had taken him only three days to get back this time. He had learned his route home. I was puzzled: how did he find this route in the first instance?

I have read about dogs and cats that have found their way back to their old homes or territory. Do they do it by smell, or by some homing sixth sense that fuddled humans do not understand. I have many talents; one of which is to get completely and hopelessly lost on new car trips. I once famously asked how far we were from our home in London just as Chris was turning the car into our drive. Did the cat have a guide dog?

I have a guide dog. He is *mon homme*. I don't have him on a leash but I walk heel to heel with him when we go walking in difficult terrains or negotiating human traffic in busy shopping streets in big cities.

"I was worried about you when you were born," my mother once said to me, "you were so fragile compared to your older sister." My older sister is 30 minutes older than me. We are twins. My mother believed that my sister had taken all the good things in the womb and I was left to survive on scraps and leftovers. My development in the first year was so slow that everybody believed I was born with a deficiency. They were right, I was born with no sense of direction. Chris absorbs my deficiency by offering his service as my official guide dog and sat-nav. Whenever we come to a T-junction, "left or right?" he would ask. Apparently a lot of male drivers ask themselves questions, shout at the traffic and swear at heaven when they are behind the wheel. Cars apparently have this stimulating effect on male hormones. Chris always turns left when I say right is right, he does it quietly, no fuss, no sneers. He knows how to show respect for my dignity.

Healey obviously had a talent that I didn't have. He had made the trip back three times, but WHY? Did he know something about this hillside that I didn't know about? I hoped this would be his last return. I hoped I would not see him on my land again. This cat seemed to have an unexplained affinity for this hill: he was determined to get back despite of the long and dangerous journey. I was getting anxious.

I remembered an old proverb on determination:

Hardship is a stone, but man's will is a hammer.

(Chinese proverb)

But I was not talking about men, I was talking about a cat.

****

Three weeks went by, with no sign of Healey. Against my will, I found myself thinking about him. It was maddening, I was looking out for HIM! One morning from the bedroom window, I saw something black moving in Chris's vineyard.

"That cat is back!" I called out excitedly.

I dashed downstairs, out of the house and straight up to the vineyard. The black something flapped into the air as I approached. A crow. Not a cat. I felt a fool, I was still in dressing gown and slippers. It was ridiculous: I had allowed a cat to infiltrate my mind. When I calmed down I realised the excitement was due to an explosion of adrenaline caused by fear. I was glad it was a crow.

A week later he really was back. We found him in profound meditation on our low garden wall. Chris picked him up, and he didn't resist. I kept a distance from both man and cat.

"This cat had taken steps to be master of his destiny," Chris said, "I admire that. We should let him stay."

"No!" my cat phobia made me shiver.

"He made the decision to return to his roots, and he's acted upon it four times. It's time we acted."

Chris started to stroke the cat.

"He has been lucky so far, his luck may run out."

"You are kind, thank you for your understanding," Healey purred softly.

"I don't want a cat in MY house, nor do I want to look over my shoulder whenever I am in the garden."

"Cats have lived on earth for many years, with and without humans. They make allowances for us."

"I've never had a cat, and I don't know how to look after one."

"He will look after himself. He is a cat."

"I will be no trouble to you, I'll find my own food and shelter. I am a cat."

Healey pushed his head into Chris's hand. Man and cat had bonded.

This was late autumn and winter was just round the corner. The weather could get very inhospitable round here. He might not make it back the fifth time. Did I want a cat's life on my conscience?

"I'll think about it. In the meantime HE stays out here and I keep all the windows and doors shut."

Without a backward glance, I went in and shut the door.

****

I thought I ought to applaud Healey's persistence and stubborn devotion to his roots. His actions struck a chord with me. I have spent most of my adult life in the west, but I feel an unbreakable bond with my native Hong Kong where all my family still live. I was very aware of what I had left behind: a loving and devoted mother and a huge extended family. I had also left behind a very tough father.

I was a weak and extremely idle child. Animals in the wild would have considered me a non viable cub, and would have abandoned or even eaten me for breakfast. My father would have had me for breakfast if he could do it without breaking the law. I grew up in perpetual fear of him, fear of ending up in his rice congee or his Mongolian hotpot. I thought I'd better get out before he found a loophole in the law to enable him to eat me up legally, and of course, the law might change to favour him. By the time I left Hong Kong, I was certain I would never get on with my father. He was the only negative reason why I left home. Wales is now my home, but Hong Kong holds my roots.

If I had been forced to leave, would I have the courage and persistence, like this cat had, to take steps to change the circumstances, to be master of my own destiny? I understand humans' attachment to their home and country, but a cat's? Healey and I were both in search of our destiny in this Welsh hillside. He seemed determined to grasp it in his paws. What about me? Would I settle and make this place my home? Would this land be my destiny? When I was young I demanded, and often succeeded in getting, answers for everything. Now I accepted the fact that not all questions had an answer. I just had to wait and see.

After only a few minutes in the garden, Healey had already stimulated a philosophical debate inside me. This cat was bad news.

4. Two Opponents.

In the days to come I found myself facing a civil war, a war of strategies and will. To lose this war would put my life into disarray.

A couple of days went by, and Healey lived in the garden. I put down clean water and a bowl of cat biscuits in a far corner, and left him to it. He never came near me, but always came over to greet Chris when he came home or went outside.

We had just finished tea in the garden when Chris said, "Look, if we are not keeping Healey, we have to get Peter to come and take him back." The cat in question was meditating on the garden wall. Chris went to bring him over, together man and cat sat opposite me, both pretending not to notice me.

I looked at the cat. It was the first time ever in my life that I got close enough to take a good look at a CAT. I saw a creature in a black fur coat, with a white front and four huge white feet. He had three daft looking white patches on his nose, that looked like a three-winged butterfly sitting off centre on his nose, though somehow he maintained his dignity in spite of it: couldn't see it, I suppose. His whiskers were long and strong, and there were lots of them. You could see them from miles on a clear day.

The truth was that he was ordinary; nothing much to look at. His green eyes were round and unblinking, unconcerned and faraway. That appealed to me; far, far away, that was where I wanted cats to be.

Healey was purring very gently, you would need a hearing aid to appreciate it. I studied him again, this time I tried to see beyond the whiskers and without prejudice; he looked serious but not fierce; contented but not obsequious; confident but low key. "He is simple and dim." Jo had been so wrong about him. Here was a cat that had proved himself to be true to his roots, tenacious and determined, a cat that believed in himself and acted to be master of his own destiny. I faced a courageous and formidable opponent.

I looked at the man. Since Healey's reappearance "the man who understands cats" had been wearing a faint and cunning smile on his face.

"The rabbits are destroying my vines, I need a cat, a good hunter to keep them down," Chris had informed me. He had started his vineyard in the field and was learning about wine making. He NEEDED a cat? Was this a plot? I faced cunning opponents.

Healey stirred in Chris's arms. I jumped.

"Keep still, you're being inspected," man said to cat.

"*I know,*" cat put a reassuring paw on man's hand. Cat purred gently. Man stroked cat. They were showing solidarity. They were trying to weaken my position!

"*Shall we go for a stroll while she makes up her mind?*" cat said to man.

"Don't worry, give her a year or two you'll have her eating out of your paw," man whispered to cat.

Chris let Healey down and hand in paw they wandered to the vineyard to discuss the job description and salary of a pest control cat.

****

My two opponents were formidable and cunning, I would exercise my wisdom and power to gain the upper hand. It was worth it! My mother would have approved.

Man and cat might be demonstrating solidarity but I knew I would have the last word. Nothing would be allowed to happen without my consent. I take pride in believing that I am one of those lucky people who are naturally suspicious. I am not easily fooled. But could I remain calm and tough in this crisis? I realised I had to choose between cowering like a disaster victim or acting like a tiger tamer.

****

I decided to keep Healey. We telephoned Peter and Jo to get their agreement. They were reluctant, but realised this was probably the best solution for the cat who kept coming back to his old territory.

Healey would be Chris's cat. I would have nothing to do with him except to feed him, OUTSIDE. The best I could do was to tolerate his existence. The cat had to observe my rules.

"Healey didn't come back for us, he came back for this land. Is that correct?"

Chris nodded. The cat blinked.

"He has invited himself to our land, so he observes our rules, is that understood?"

"They are your rules. I have no rules for cats. And remember, he was here first," Chris said.

"*I was born and bred here. I am Welsh, you two are foreigners. This is my land.*" Cat's whiskers twitched confidently. Man nodded in agreement.

I ignored them and announced my rules, "He must not try to be friendly with me. He must stay at least six feet away from me at all times. There is no popping up from behind shrubs to give me a nice surprise." (Memo to self: mustn't do anything stupid, like being nice to him.)

"He lives outside, under no circumstances is he allowed into the house." (Memo: must remember to shut ALL windows and doors at all times.)

"What? Even in bad weather! That's a bit heartless," Chris sounded disgusted. (Reminder: don't give in to criticism, all negotiations must start from the lowest position.)

"He feeds on what he catches, and I will feed him occasionally, with table scraps only. No spoiling!"

There was no reminder here. I couldn't use poverty as an excuse not to buy cat food. Chris's approach to housekeeping is, "I make the money, you spend it," and meanness is not his weak point.

Two big question marks appeared in the cat's eyes. *"I already do all those things. Why is she stating the obvious?"* the cat meowed.

"She doesn't understand cats, you'll teach her, you cats are good teachers," man replied. "It will be an interesting experience for both of you," he added, smiling.

"This is not a joke," I said, "I am doing both of you a big favour. I expect you to respect my authority and observe my rules." Chris smiled.

I would feed and water him and nothing else. No matter what happened he had to take care of them himself.

I would endeavour to put a thousand obstacles between him and me and another thousand between him and my home. When faced with a thousand rejections, would this cat still keep his calm nerve? I would see. I could quote hundreds of wise men to support my actions, here is one of them.

When granting a favour, make it meagre at first and more generous later;
Do it the other way round, and people will forget what you've given.
When imposing authority, be strict at first and lenient later;

Do it the other way round, and people will resent your harshness.

(Hung Ying-ming)

5. A Cool Cat.

Know yourself and know your enemy, you win a hundred battles;
Know yourself but not your enemy, you have a 50 to 50 chance of victory;
Know not yourself and know not your enemy you lose every battle.

(Sun Tse)

How would I go about defeating an enemy I knew nothing about? My predicament reminded me of the above saying from *The Art of War,* written by Sun Tse, a military genius and warfare strategist who lived during the Warring States period (475-221 BC).

Healey wasn't my only problem.

It was the beginning of my second year in rural Wales and I was a bit unhappy. I had spent most of my adult life in Hong Kong and later London, and city culture was in my blood. From day one after moving here, Chris was received into a social circle in his work place. I went straight into a social vacuum, and found myself alone most of the day.

Being alone has never bothered me. Most painters are solitary souls and I like to work in a reclusive environment. The problems arose outside my working hours. Friends were now a two and a half hour train journey away. All the conveniences and familiarities of a well loved city had disappeared overnight. "What am I doing here?" was a question I kept asking myself.

My dream of a peaceful and quiet life in the country didn't work out as I had hoped. Chris worked hard, days and often nights. He had professional business in London which required him to be away a lot. He loved his work in the

20

hospital and he strived to do his best for his professional body. I spent more time alone.

We had been so busy planning the move, then the move. Once here we worked to make the house habitable. The process was disrupted and greatly delayed by a disconnected water pipe in the ceiling of the ground floor toilet. The whole ground floor flooded. For six months we lived in the cold and damp with humidifiers on full blast 24/7 to dry the walls and floors. I had not given a moment of thought as to what living here would be like. Then Chris started serious on call duty in the hospital and began to stay away on his various College duties. The silence in the house was overwhelming. The garden became unfriendly with this evil beast around. The full implication of this new life hit.

During some of its worst moments, I found comfort in re-reading the ancient Chinese classics; and stimulation in painting Wales in Chinese styles, mainly in the company of dull weather and the silence. I understood merely surviving was not enough. I had to embrace this new life because Chris and I had made this decision together. I probably sounded very ungrateful for the good things: the beautiful countryside, the nice big house, the wonderful and successful husband, but the feeling of dislocation was powerful and real. I had to make a meaningful life for myself all over again. How? I had no idea. And there was this cat in my garden! I didn't smile for a year.

I learnt fast as I strove to make sense of my new life. Two lessons have stood out. I learn that winters can last up to 20 months in the country; that power cuts happen in the darkest of days and nights, often when you are alone in the house when the only other occupant is 200 miles away; that the cut comes with no warning and can last from 3 seconds to 3 days; that your saving grace is the humble candle, which is your only source of light and warmth. I learn to deal with my fear, often alone, of total darkness (no street lights here) and the unknown great outdoors in stormy weather and heavy snow.

I learn to deal with bats. I read about them and saw them in paintings, but never in real life, that was before I came to Wales. I would never imagine that these tiny mouse look-alikes with wings would arouse such strong emotions in me. The first time when a bat strayed into the kitchen I completely freaked out. I became so tense I nearly shattered the glass of wine I was holding in my hand. I screamed and I screamed: Chris thought an alarm had gone off. The flying mouse was doing its ghost flight above our heads, completely silent. *"Ha, I've got you!"* its radar signalled. With great common sense and the highest level of diplomacy on Chris's part, like opening all windows to the outside and turning off all inside lights, we managed to, respectfully, persuade our unwelcome guest that a humble country kitchen like ours was no place for it and that it should leave us to get on with our cooking. It flew around for a while longer, just so we knew who was in charge, and left voluntarily. We didn't intimidate or threaten it with violence. We know if a bat reports us to its protection body we will be in great trouble with the law. Bats are protected by laws and they have more rights to be in your house than you have. They can instruct their lawyers to sue you (note to bat protection authorities: this is a joke).

I have learnt two things that night: I have a high note that a soprano might kill for; and I am terrified of bats. I fear cats but I am terrified of bats.

It wasn't all doom and gloom. These experiences and encounters have taught me something about myself; that I am tougher than I thought. But I still couldn't cope with this cat in the garden!

Healey's constant presence magnified my unhappiness tenfold. Cat phobia had been with me all my life, it was part of my mental makeup, almost an ally. I was comfortable with it. There was nothing shameful about being frightened of cats, after all, Alexander the Great, Napoleon and Genghis Khan were cat phobic. I was interested to read that Napoleon loved dogs but would break into a cold sweat at even the sight of a kitten. See what they had achieved in spite of it – or because of it?

Chinese folk legends are graced with stories of cats and famous historical figures, combining fictional imagination and realistic description of historical facts. My personal favourite is the story about cat and Confucius, our great philosopher and teacher.

Confucius was playing the zither in his study. As usual a few of his disciples were outside listening. They were puzzled by what they heard. Instead of the subtle, harmonious and serene melodies that Confucius usually played, the tune was melancholy, its mood at times haunting, at times slow and grinding, and at times compelling. It built up to a crescendo and ended in a bleak mood.

The disciples entered the study and asked for an explanation. Confucius smiled and explained, "I have just witnessed a cat stalking a mouse. The cat moved slowly and cautiously, it was completely silent but I felt tension and danger in the air. Then it pounced and caught its prey. The killing had affected my mood, hence the tune."

See how these beasts can affect even the greatest!

****

"What will this domesticated cat do to me?" I asked myself. I had no answer. Ask anyone who is frightened of bats or butterflies the same question, they would have no answer either. If we had, phobia would acquire a different status in the medical dictionary, it would become a rational and real fear. I had always been able to avoid cats and contain my phobia effectively. Now I had to confront it head on. In a moment of madness, I had allowed this cat to come into my radar space, to threaten my comfort zone. I was living in constant fear of this beast. I became very angry with myself, with Chris and above all, with the cat. I lived in a serious red alert state. In the garden I constantly looked over my shoulder to see if he was stalking me. His unwavering and steady gaze sent shivers down my spine. Leisure strolls in the garden were possible only when my cat tamer was about. All essential gardening jobs were done in a rush because this damned cat had cultivated a habit of crouching six feet away from wherever I was working. When I went inside I looked over my shoulder to make sure he wasn't following me into the house. I shut all the windows even on hot days in case he sneaked in. This cat had turned my life into a misery. His presence made me sick and anxious. This black shadow was constantly at my heel. He had made me a prisoner in my own home. There has to be a support group out there, or a website that helps people who are imprisoned in their own home by a psychotic cat. When you go to get a dog or cat, you choose, but I was chosen. He had come with his own name, and a CV I never read. He had demonstrated tremendous skills in stalking me. He could be a serial killer.

Sometimes I'd looked out into the night and saw this dark shape sitting there, on his haunches, menacing and motionless, like the stone statue that guarded the tombs of ancient Chinese Emperors. Occasionally he moved his head like a revolving security camera, following me with his evil eyes. I shut all curtains.

What I needed most was a very special friend, someone who understood solitude, aloneness and rural existence, to miraculously connect me to my new environment, and to share with me the beauty and goodness of country life. I needed a companion who was mostly silent and looked elegant enough to match the Welsh landscape, and tactful enough not to interrupt the flow of the breeze and the bees.

"Get a Doberman or a Bull Dog the size of a gorilla, they will have the cat for breakfast," a dog lover friend suggested. I didn't want Healey to end his life as dog food. I only wanted him to go away.

To be fair Healey did not barge in on my life. Instead he pursued me with silent dignity. He hovered on the perimeter, pretending to be unaware of me. He followed me around in the garden, but never got too close to alarm me. He would sit for hour upon hour on the garden wall, and would lift his head to look at me as I passed him.

He looked good natured but he still had very long curved claws and too many sharp and spiky teeth. His persistence irritated me. Here I was in my home conducting a silent war, with a stubborn cat who didn't know there was a war on. I could feel his palpable strength. The frightening thing was I didn't understand cats but this cat seemed to understand me.

"*I come in peace,*" he purred his silent purr.

"You have a ploy in your cunning heart but you won't win," I yelled at him from six feet away.

"*Why are you so uncertain about me?*" he meowed.

"This is not personal. My uncertainty lies with all cats."

He started to lick his fur.

"What compels him to stay despite my rejection?" I asked Chris.

"He loves you," he said.

"I do not wish to be loved by any cat! And what do they know about love?"

"*We know a lot about love, and we don't give it away too cheaply, like dogs do,*" Healey blinked.

"My love, there is nothing shameful about being loved by a cat," Chris gave me a big hug, "try to understand him and learn to like him."

Learn to like a cat! How ridiculous. It was not difficult to be angry and assertive to ugly and aggressive beasts, the problem was that Healey was such a gentle and reasonable soul. I had a cool cat on my hands. I had to find a way to increase my chances of driving him to leave voluntarily.

I knew myself: I was a hard-core cat phobic. Chris was right: I knew nothing about cats. I started to read cat books.

The truth was I had begun to develop an unfortunate interest in Healey, like that of a woman who wants to know more about a man and knows she shouldn't.

Why did I allow myself to get so entangled with this cat? And how could he stay so cool?

6. Life of A Sage.

The wise cautiously goes along with what is inevitable,
While the foolish resist and blindly fight.

(Chinese proverb)

Healey continued to behave impeccably, never complained, never threw a tantrum over my treatment of him.

"Oh, roast chicken, that is awfully nice of you," Healey purred softly as I put his food down on the gravel. I stood away as he ate standing up. We had roast chicken for dinner. I carved a slice from the breast, then another, for him.

"He was working really hard in your vineyard today," I said to Chris.

"One is enough for him, I like chicken breast too!" Chris yelled. Was there a faint smile on his face? I was getting soft. I had tried to justify myself: Healey had earned his chicken.

We had had a problem with rabbits in the field. They had chewed the vine saplings and wiped out the leafy vegetables. That was before Healey took up the job as pest control officer. Since his return the rabbit population in our field had dropped significantly. I had seen him running down the garden path from the vineyard, with a fully grown, very dead rabbit hanging from his teeth. He ran with his head up so as not to trip over the body. A few birds twittered by and Healey didn't waver. I watched as he jumped over the field fence into the garden, down the lawn and down the low wall towards the garage. All the time he held the rabbit firmly between his teeth. Skilfully and elegantly he negotiated his way without dropping his catch. He glanced briefly at my direction, his big green eyes focused and remote. He didn't notice me, I wasn't there. He was no longer the stalker I feared, no longer a docile pet. He was a hunter, a killer. He was a descendant of the tiger. Something moved me; his concentration and his confidence. The proud hunter had returned with his catch.

If you see someone most days of the week, sooner or later this person will become a fixture in your radar. Soon you learn that your postman is called Jamie, he takes every Tuesday off and he has a wife and three children. You learn that your village postmaster is called Gareth and that his breath smells of his cigarettes. One year on I was beginning to tolerate Healey. He had made sure that I saw him everyday. He had asserted himself as a fixture in my radar, this cunning beast. It didn't mean I was comfortable with him, but the severe red alert was downgraded to red alert. I still took all the necessary safeguards when he was around. I let him into the kitchen to feed, but only when Chris was around (as a backup in case of sudden panic on my part).

Otherwise he was fed outside, even when it rained or snowed. Very quickly he learnt that breakfast was around seven in the morning, and dinner around eight in the evening. At the appointed time he would magically appear on the garden wall, sitting facing the kitchen window. His face was a picture of patience, like a restaurant diner waiting quietly for his overdue order, not wanting to upset the staff by complaining.

During a particularly heavy shower we tried holding an umbrella over him to keep the rain off his food. He looked at the brolly as if it was the sky falling on his head. It appeared the brolly was not appropriate.

"Don't worry about me, I am a cat, I am waterproof."

"No, the brolly is not for you, it's for us. We humans are not waterproof," I said.

He ran off, and didn't return for his food that night. Soon after that I took pity on him, and full time indoor eating began. He ate by the kitchen door, and was let out as soon as he finished. He might have many tricks and ploys up his paws but I was in charge. I could not cope with a cat wandering around in the house.

I was beginning to feel guilty. Why was I raging a war against a cat that had proved to be totally harmless? The rejections and steps I put up against him were driven by fear and self preservation. The cat phobia had stripped me of all my common sense.

"He is all right, he has shelter, food and freedom to roam. He has everything he needs. He seems happy enough," Chris said.

Confucius said to his disciples, *"Eat coarse rice, drink cold water, use my bent arm as a pillow: there is happiness in all these."*

Happy? Maybe. According to the great Master, Healey was living the life of an ancient sage.

****

Healey lived an outdoor existence for over a year. In bad weather he took shelter under anything he could find, like cars and garden benches. His favourite was the little stone table made out of an old paving stone supported on either side by two rectangular stone blocks. I called it Stonehenge. It was sited on the elevated part of the garden directly facing the kitchen window. He would sit there and watch me going about my kitchen jobs. I could see him watching me, his big round eyes alight with meaning. I didn't look long enough to work out what the meaning was.

"It is friendship! Try blinking at him, he would like that," Chris said. Blinking at a cat, what a mad idea!

One afternoon I stepped out into the garden after a good morning's work in my studio. I was tired but satisfied. The sky was blue. The flowers were in full bloom and I could smell the freshly cut grass. I felt happy and generous. Healey was looking at me on the garden wall. I decided to blink at him. I stood six feet away and blinked. He stared at me with two big question marks in his eyes. I got closer, took a big breath and blinked again. This time I called his name softly. He didn't blink back at me, instead he rolled over on his back and purred softly with his eyes half shut. This was extraordinary, he was showing me his belly. What was I to do with it? He stretched his front legs and I saw the claws. I felt goose pimples all over me. I walked away quietly.

Healey slept in the roof space of the stable barn where he was born. We subsequently bought the barn and converted half of it into a garage. The other half remained as a stable.

"The roof space gives me shelter and the sweet smelling straw keeps me warm and comfortable." That was what the cat told the Man. I had never gone up in the roof space and had no intention of doing so. Healey could sleep anywhere as long as it was outside.

"The roof space is primitive, and is not wind proof. Get the cat inside for the winter, for goodness sake!" my friend Ingrid shouted at me down the phone when I told her about the roof.

Ingrid lives alone with two cats (current whisker count) in a suburban street on the outskirts of north London. She has had cats all her life. Part-time consultant to the unofficial abandoned cat welfare society, she often drags herself into the lives of stray cats. She is the official godmother to all the cats on her street because she always offers to look after her neighbours' cats when they go on holiday. In spite of an active social life with humans and other cats she makes time to spoil her own cats outrageously.

"The less you try to impose your will on them and the less you restrain them, the happier you both are." This is her motto.

"H knows sufficiency, and he has a thick fur coat. The roof may be primitive but so is a cat. He is all right," I said.

"This is disgraceful, you are utterly heartless! Big H deserves someone better."

Ingrid regards herself as the true professional cat woman, the rests are amateurs.

Well, as far as I was concerned, if H didn't like it he could always pack up and go back to live with his mother. A lot of men do that when they have an argument with their girl friends.

Did I call him H? Did Ingrid also call him H? When did I give him this pet name?

I was very aware that I was seeing this cat everyday. I had to be careful, one day he might end up becoming a part of my life. I was already dealing with a big change. I didn't want any disruption, especially not from an uninvited cat from outer space. I decided to continue treating him with cool respect and from a great distance. In other words I continued to reject him. He had to sleep outside, in the open, under the stars and the moon. The kind of life that many sages in ancient time aspired to.

There was nothing disgraceful with the way I treated the cat.

7. The Adoption.

It was Healey's second winter with us. It was a bad one with sub-zero temperatures and snow on the ground most of the time. One week in January Chris went to London for a few days. The day after he left it started to snow heavily. Healey did not turn up for his feed. I went out looking for him, calling and banging his food bowl. Soon the snow turned into a blizzard. I became desperate to find him. The desperation was driven by conscience and responsibility, not connection or love, I told myself. I got our neighbour John to come and help, we got the ladder, and I climbed up to the roof space in the stable to see if he was there. He wasn't. Standing on the top of the ladder I could feel the bitter north wind blowing into the space. This was no shelter for any living thing, primitive or noble. There was no sweet smelling hay but a handful of thin straw. Healey had been sleeping on bare roof board for over a year! I felt very ashamed.

On my way back to the house I heard a faint meow. It had come from under my car which now looked like a gigantic Christmas cake, buried in snow. I followed the sound and called his name. He meowed louder. Pushing away the snow from under the car I found H.

"Do you like my igloo?" he meowed soulfully. I was so relieved that I felt like picking him up and hugging him, though I still couldn't.

"Time you had some food," I said.

I walked ahead of him, making a track in the snow with my Wellingtons. He followed. I couldn't let him eat in the house as my protector was not at home. I cleared the snow off the kitchen windowsill, put a big plate of food there and waited. Healey jumped up and started eating immediately. I watched him in silence. His face full of concentration, he ate slowly, standing up. His big feet looked even bigger on the snow. I helped steady his food plate with one hand, with the other I started stroking him gently. His fur felt so smooth and thick. It was the first time I had touched a cat without thick gloves on. He pushed his head up to meet my hand briefly and then slowly he sat down to eat, his tail lying flat behind him. He emptied his food plate, jumped off the window sill and looked up at me. His green eyes looked clear and bright against the snow. He looked me in the eyes, then slowly he walked away, towards his igloo. At that moment I felt something had happened between me and this cat; for the first time we had made a connection, a two way connection.

That evening I fed him in the kitchen. Chris telephoned from his London hotel and we had a long chat. I told him what had happened and he was very pleased to hear that Healey was in the kitchen as we spoke. Shortly after the phone call there was a power cut. The whole house was plunged into complete darkness. The heavy snow had brought down the power lines. It is something that happens not infrequently where we live. We are well prepared for it. Moving cautiously I found and lit an oil lamp and a couple of candles. Suddenly I remembered the cat.

"H, where are you?" I was beginning to panic.

"I am right here." The meow came from under a chair. He had his tail and all four paws tucked under the thick fur coat. He glanced up at me as if to say, *"Are you all right?"* He was a picture of calm and gentleness. I was alone with H, without my tiger tamer.

"H, you should be somewhere where you can sit in front of a fire, drink whisky and smoke a cigar. You shouldn't be here. I don't deserve you."

"I don't smoke and I don't drink, I am a cat," he blinked, *"and I decide who deserves me because …… "*

"Yes, I know, because you are a cat," I finished his words for him. Where was my fear now? The whole thing seemed so absurd and unreal.

Then I thought, "What if he wants to go out? How will I know?" I remembered reading a cat column in the paper, when someone wrote and asked just that question: "How will I know?" The answer was, "You will know!" Would I know? How? I worried about it.

Then H showed me. When the time came, he walked to the back door. He looked at the handle. They were right: I knew. *"Time I was out."* Dogs have owners, cats have staff, I remembered.

I opened the door, we both stepped outside. The air was bitterly cold, a shiver went down my spine. The snow had stopped, a big moon shone brightly, lighting the snow-capped garden. I stood there absorbing the beauty of it, momentarily forgetting the cat by my feet. Seconds later, I looked down. I was alone. Healey had gone.

At that moment I knew that this gentle and wise creature in a black fur coat had won.

Exercise gentleness, you will subdue harshness;

Exercise gentleness with wisdom, you will overcome the most powerful resistance.

(Feng Menglong)

****

A week after the snow storm Healey became the proud owner of his own studio flat. Chris built a cat flap in the garage door. In its roof space I put down a piece of carpet, on it I put a thick box stuffed with a multiple layers of straw. By the side I put a bowl of milk, and cat biscuits. What was missing was a bottle of brandy and a picture of a lost love. I had wanted to put in a power shower and a fitted kitchen. Chris thought it would not really be appreciated. I didn't argue, I know who the boss is when it comes to Do It Yourself projects in our household. Within minutes, the proud owner had moved in.

The weeks passed by and there was no let-up in his affection. I became more confident in his presence. He came to eat in the kitchen, and was allowed to stay in the dining room while we had our dinner.

H was apprehensive the first time he came into the dining room. He sniffed around cautiously. The investigation stopped at the radiator. It was blasting out heat and the carpet under it was very warm. H looked up, I swore he was smiling. I swore I saw a light bulb go on over his big head. He looked lovingly and deeply into the carpet, dropped on it and rolled on it. He serenaded it with his gentle deep purr, like that of a baritone serenading his lover. *"It is a lot warmer than my studio flat, thank you so much,"* he grinned at me. I went over and sat down by him at about two feet away. For a brief moment we gazed at each other.

"I know you have a decision to make," his gaze seemed to say. We both knew whatever it was it would be for life. Then he settled down to sleep on his back with his four big feet up, supporting the radiator, his new true love. Chris had been watching us quietly. Didn't he say something to the cat, like, "give her a year and she will eat out of your paw." It had taken H almost a year and a half to achieve this. When chucking out time came he reluctantly bid farewell to his new found love.

"Can I stay a bit longer?" he asked.

"No. I give you an inch and you want a mile. OUT!"

Soon we let him into the sitting room. There he found his second love: Chris's lap. Man and cat would sit watching TV together. Then the cat would start snoring, to be followed shortly by the man.

Three weeks after he was allowed into the house Chris built a cat flap into the porch, with my full (only slightly nervous) approval. Healey could come and go as he wished.

I was developing a warm but cautious affection for Healey. I no longer feared him, but I still became anxious when he got too close. Somewhere in his psyche he seemed to know that I was different from Chris and his former family, and that he must treat this *difference* with respect. He knew I needed space and he was generous in his giving.

He still watched me, and would often glance up at me and blink. I responded by calling him softly, dragging his name out "H-e-a-l-e-y". This seemed to give him great pleasure as he would purr gently, and roll over.

The impossible had happened: a cat had successfully adopted me and I felt good about it.

What is believed to be inevitable may not happen;
What appears to be impossible sometimes occurs.

(Chinese proverb)

8. Partner at Work.

Slowly I adapted to rural life, and began the task of building a life for myself. Painting is a way of life for me, and is by nature a solitary activity. These days I was no longer allowed to be alone. H would wander into my studio, he would sit there, dozing, meditating, having beautiful thoughts or just reading the carpet (he would sit with his head down, looking just like a sage deciphering a difficult text).

The first time I introduced him to my studio he showed a great interest in everything.

"Wow! This is pure heaven."

He didn't wait a second before getting on with what cats are best at; being inquisitive.

He sniffed, pushed, pawed and sniffed again at everything. There were lots of objects for him to explore; the sweet smell of Chinese ink; Chinese colours in tubes, in powder and in paste; painting brushes made of hair from wolf, sheep and mountain horses. He loved the rolls of Chinese papers; Moon Palace, Single Suan, Double Suan, and hand made bark paper, just to name a few. I threw him a few old pieces and he would immediately shred them to bits.

I am a very tidy person and I usually tidy my work rooms when I finish a painting project, which usually takes a year to 18 months. On this particular occasion I was doing a commission work; to paint, in Chinese style, the famous castles and architectural sites in Wales. I was half way into this project. There were sketches and references everywhere, on my big table, on chairs, on the floor, and there was more in the big wastepaper bin. It was a good time to introduce H to my work room. He could see it all, at first hand, what a no nonsense and tidy person I was.

He had been working at the bin of scrap paper and failed sketches. He pulled a piece out, sniffed it, held it between his paws and shred it to bits with his teeth. I felt a slight panic when I saw his claws and teeth in action.

"Do you make a living doing this?"

"No."

"Is it why you send the man out to work?"

"Yes."

Art these days (always?) is about salesmanship, publicity, promotion and the occasional shock tactic. I have no such support systems or inclination. I paint for myself. Although I don't do any self promotion, I am not shy about my work. I show them to the public and put a price on them. If people like them enough as to part with their money, it is a bonus for me. What I do is not about chasing wealth and celebrity, it is the satisfaction and pride that comes with creating something that I consider beautiful.

H yawned, all this art stuff was too much for his tiny brain, he went to sit under the long window, gave himself a wash all over and went to sleep. That became his favourite spot. There he would lounge, look at the world outside and snooze, he knew that I was there in the same room with him. He was contented.

When I called his name he would come and lie close to me without touching me. Once in a while he would roll over, stretch his arms out as if to invite me to pull his whiskers and scratch his ears. I always declined. While he seemed to demonstrate complete trust in me, I still felt uncertain. His calm and silent presence graced my studio, and his all too obvious contentment rubbed off on me. I had discovered the joy of sharing my space with a cat.

Wales is an inspiration for painters. Everywhere you look there is always something beautiful to sketch. I started painting the Welsh landscape in Chinese style. It culminated in solo exhibitions, and the commission to paint castles in

Wales. I set up a class to teach Chinese brush painting (now in its 15th year!)

What next? I got restless. I do not need a reason to paint, the process of painting is reward and happiness itself. But I do need to explore new ground frequently, to paint something that would require me to learn and to solve problems. I paint everyday. It is a matter of "keep learning, keep studying, keep growing."

It was a warm spring morning. I was planting bulbs in the rockery. Healey was lazing around. These days he followed me everywhere in the garden. *"I want to be your shadow,"* he purred.

I stopped for a rest. Looking around I saw my SHADOW fast asleep at the top end of the rockery. He was next to my own version of a garden gnome; a laughing Buddha statue. The scene caught my attention. I watched as cat slept and Buddha laughed, totally unaware of the birds singing around them. How serene and calm they looked! Cat slept soundly, dreaming of his proud and splendid past. Buddha's big grin was kindly and unfathomable, perhaps mocking the material world.

There were interesting contrasts too: soft fur versus hard stone; snoring cat versus laughing Buddha; dainty paws and solid carved hands; wild feline pride and gentle Buddha grace; God's creation versus man-made object. A bird twittered by and Healey stirred. He opened his eyes and yawned, before going back to sleep with his front paws around Buddha's shoulder. My mind was working fast. I was already composing mental images of cat paintings. I had found my stimulus.

I started painting cats. It was a very steep learning curve, as I had never painted cats before. I studied cat movements, using Healey as my model. I also took an interest in other people's cats, observing and sketching them. Su Dongpo (1037-1101), one of China's greatest poets and painters, had this advice to painters: *Before you set out to paint a bamboo, you must study it until you have all its details in your mind.* I sketched and read enough cat books to warrant a Master's degree in Cat Studies. My fear of cats, strangely, had got less with more exposure (Chris says, Yes, that's how they treat phobias).

Putting aside skills and techniques, two factors determine the quality of my work: attention to details and respect for the subject matter. The first factor requires persistence and discipline. I usually work at an object every day in order to produce accurate details, so I spent days on ends sketching and drawing cats.

But to respect cats? where would I begin, I asked myself. Without respect my painting has no life, because my painting is but a dead reproduction of the body, without the soul. I was surprised at how easy it was to say to H, "Yes, I have a lot of respect for you. I have learnt to understand you." This respect has come from my observation of cats: they have their own talents and folly, their own view on life with their own set of responses. And the few exceptional ones, like H, also have sensitivity and moral courage.

It was a task that would take me almost two years to complete. I painted cats in all weather and in all moods. I painted them in Chinese styles, and matched each painting with Chinese sayings. A year later, my first book of paintings and quotes, *The Cat and the Tao*, was published.

I realised I was slowly assimilating this cat into my life and my heart. I hadn't expected to build up this level of trust. I was pleased to have been able to do so.

My attitude towards my cat had changed. Fear had grown into admiration, resistance had turned into acceptance, and indifference had turned into affection.

9. Two Kittens.

Healey turned out to be a high maintenance cat. He had a chronic skin condition caused by flea allergy. During severe attacks he would scratch and lick until there was hardly any fur left in his abdomen and inside of his legs. Bits of his black fur were turning a reddish brown through constant licking.

"Will he die from this?" I asked the doctor of the house.

"Skin allergy doesn't cause death, this applies to both humans and animals. There is a long distance between them, and there is treatment," Chris explained.

Healey required regular vet care. Chris and I spent an arm and a leg in the process. Vets do not undervalue their services, and we never begrudge what we pay. "Veterinary medicine is a lot cheaper than human private medicine," Chris says.

Finally the vet put him on a long acting steroid injection. The treatment reduced the inflammation and it kept the allergy under control. Healey stopped scratching and his fur began to grow back. He would need long term care, life wouldn't be perfect for him, nor for me. We both had to learn to accept and live with his condition.

One day H didn't come in for his breakfast. I went out looking for him and found him wandering in the garden looking confused and disorientated. His eyes were unfocused and expressionless. We took him to the vet immediately. He had a serious form of enteritis, and was in a "touch and go" situation. He was quietly drifting away. The vet kept him in for intensive care, and we were told to prepare for the worst. I couldn't put into words how I felt, knowing that he might not come home.

****

He made a full recovery from the enteritis. It took his illness to make me realise just how much H meant to me. I would never forget the joy I felt the moment when Chris and I went to the surgery to fetch him home.

"H, promise me you will tell me when you don't feel well." I was worried. The cat books tell me that sick cats will often seek out and hide in a quiet spot to die.

"*But how?*"

"Oh, I don't know," I scratched my head, "what about rubbing the sore part with one paw, and use both paws if the pain is really bad, and try screaming out loud. This is what most humans do."

"*I don't complain, I am a cat.*"

This episode affected both of us. We spent more time together. He started to keep me under constant surveillance, and would not let me out of his sight. When I took the rubbish out, he came along too, wanting to know where I was going, WHO was in the bags and what I was doing with them.

He seemed to be saying to me: "*I may not be with you much longer, I hope you will remember me when I am gone.*"

H was a great success in keeping the rabbits down. Chris gave some thought to succession planning, and decided to recruit more cats for his vineyard.

"You must train up more staff before you retire!" he told the cat. The cat looked at me soulfully, and I looked at the man fiercely, "No way! over Healey's dead body," I said.

Healey wasn't the only creature round here on four legs, who wore a fur coat and had a tail. There were the two pedigree chocolate brown Labradors; Emperor Maximillian (aka Max) and Empress Isabella (aka Bella). There was HRH Prince Coco and his sister HRH Princess Lily. They were pedigree aristocrats from the Royal Court of old Burma.

And then there was Joshua, a regal ginger tom cat, a real life gladiator. Joshua lived to fight and to win, but he chose his opponents. He had never fought those that lived in the hamlet. Joshua's illustrious life deserved to be told in a separate book. These distinguished creatures were the live-in companions of Ruth and her daughter Mabel. They lived in a palace disguised as a listed farm house.

Then there were the non-royals; Ben and Rose, brother and sister domestic short-hair, farm cats, and their companion Sweep, a rescued sheep dog. They lived with Claire, our other neighbour.

So H was not short of company if he wanted any. He could pick his friends as well as enemies. He didn't bother with them because he was contented. He only wanted me and he knew he had me in his paws.

"Look at his face, he is depressed, bored and fed up." Chris picked H up, sat him on his lap to face me, so that I could see what a depressed cat looked like. "Listen, you can hear him sigh. He needs a playmate."

Healey looked the same to me, a serious looking cat with serious thoughts, dignified and inscrutable. These qualities are often interpreted as toughness and strength in humans. Many successful and powerful men have this look. If H was a politician he would be the one that would save the world and would not say a word about it afterwards.

"He doesn't need a playmate. He has got me; his soul mate," I said to Chris.

"H, do you want a playmate? This is your chance." I bent down to stroke him.

"Oh, push off, give me a break," he stared at me and then jumped off Chris's lap.

"Chris, you are right, H is depressed," I concluded. I recognised a depressed cat when I heard one.

Did he pretend to be happy, when in all likelihood he was depressed? But why, he roamed the land freely and he had an attentive and devoted servant?

I conceded, it might not be a bad idea for Healey to have other cats' company.

I went further with the idea. I suggested that we should get a couple of pedigree cats, breed them and sell them. In a few years time we might make enough money for Chris to stop his medical work, and I could stop painting.

"Then what do we do?" he laughed.

"We can spend the rest of our lives getting bored and arguing with each other, and breeding cats."

I knew, more cats meant I would need to adapt, and H would need to make compromises.

****

Friends suggested that we went to the local cat sanctuary to get our cats. I declined because I suspected that Chris might come home with half a dozen cats. Some emailed us web sites where we could buy pedigree cats with royal blood. I didn't want that either. I wouldn't know how to care for royals. We couldn't afford their life style or provide them with Special Branch round the clock protection.

We went to see a couple of kittens in a local residential home for adults with learning difficulties, run by a friend's mother. A pregnant cat had taken up residence there, and had given birth to three kittens; two toms and a tortoiseshell queen. They were four weeks old and needed a home. The staff had decided to keep the mother cat.

"*I believe we have met before,*" the mother cat said to "the man who understands cats" when we arrived. She sat on his lap the minute he sat down.

"*Look at my kittens, aren't they beautiful,*" she said, purring for Wales as Chris stroked her gently.

On the floor were three little creatures, hardly bigger than stag beetles.

An all black kitten with a tiny white bow tie was looking up the back of a huge sofa. Like a philosopher, he was in serious contemplation, pondering what it was like to be so tall and big. And whether he could climb up there!

The tortoiseshell kitten was small and dainty, but she had been spoken for. She was sitting there serenely like a film star, her vanity bag packed, waiting for her chauffeur driven limousine. Her serenity didn't last long.

The third kitten had different ideas. He decided to have a go at her. He threw himself at her, whacked her with a swift right cross to the jaw, wrestled her to the floor and started to beat her up furiously with his tiny paws. The girl screamed and yelled, *"I've no papa and mama is busy talking to that man, will somebody please help me!"*

Everybody laughed, I didn't. This SAS commando had a black fur with a white shirt front and random white patches. He was another post-office cat, a Healey look alike, but with none of Healey's cool and calm manner.

These little devils had demonstrated minds and personalities of their own. At this young age they seemed to have already carved out careers for themselves; a philosopher, a film star and a commando: pretty illustrious for a family of cats.

It was the first time I had been in the same room with kittens. I stood near the door ready for a quick get away! I could feel goose pimples all over, and my semi-dormant fear of cats was rising to the surface. Then the unthinkable happened.

"Come and hold this one."

Chris came towards me with the all-black philosopher in his hands. My blood froze. All eyes were on me. I wished a trapdoor would open under my feet, plunge me down and send me cart-wheeling back to my house. It didn't happen. I wasn't going to let myself down. I took a few deep breaths and took the kitten from Chris's hands. *"Don't you drop my boy!"* his mother's voice came from somewhere.

I held him nervously. He felt very soft and boneless. He stared at me with his big eyes, they looked inquisitive and fearless! He wriggled, I tightened my hold, he nibbled my fingers, I dropped him. Chris was waiting, caught him as he fell, and gently put him down. The philosopher immediately went to his mother and meowed, *"did you see that, she almost dropped ME!"*

They say that small pets are excellent companions, they help lower blood pressure and improve physical and mental health. After fifteen minutes with these three, I could feel my blood pressure shooting out of my ears!

Chris wanted both toms. I reluctantly agreed. "I am much bigger than the pair of them put together. If I wanted to I could beat the daylights out of them with a broomstick!" Those were my parting thoughts.

We planned to pick them up five weeks later, when they were nine weeks, but a week later the staff rang to say that the kittens were running onto the street, and they were too busy to keep an eye on them. Also, the residents wanted the windows open because it was warm. The kittens might get run over, they said. Could we collect them earlier?

We went the next day. We drove home with two five week old kittens in one cat basket. The SAS commando protested during the whole journey. He threatened to blow us up with a hand grenade if we didn't return him to his mother immediately. We called him Joseph. The philosopher sat at the back, contemplating life in a basket. We called him Rocco.

A Chinese proverb says: *Characteristics shown at three years old are unlikely to change at eighty*: three years? Five weeks, if you're a kitten!

A friend had suggested that we should get a girl. "A nice young female would lift the old boy out of his depression. A rush of testosterone, that's what H needs," she said.

I know the type; middle-aged men who can't and won't cope with life. They seek comfort in the bosoms of younger women, hoping to bring back their lost youth. But there were not girls available, so we came home with two boys.

10. A Few Things about Kittens.

The less you know the more confident you are.

(Confucius)

I had thought that H had taught me everything I needed to know about cats, so I was cautiously confident about taking on the two kittens. In the days to come, I was to learn that my initial confidence was based on ignorance, not knowledge. I had a lot more to learn.

The first thing I had to find out about was cat litter. Yes, I did say cat litter. Healey had introduced me to the world of cat food; Whiskers, Go-Cat, Felix and many other brands. He embraced them all providing I threw in the odd plate of roast meat, smoked salmon sandwich and prawn cocktail. H was never fussy about his food.

H didn't teach me anything about cat litter. He made full use of the gigantic portaloo which I called the great outdoors. I had seen him peeing at the top of the field while I was sketching a mental image of the valley down below. I had seen him relieving himself under the fragrant wisteria while humming a song to a bumble bee. Chris and I once stayed in a family run hotel in Ireland. It boasted an en-suite room with a bathroom almost good enough to sell the house by itself; it commanded the most spectacular view of western Ireland. We paid £200 a night for the privilege. Healey had his for free.

"Healey, did you use a cat litter tray when you were a kitten?" I asked the cat.

"What's cat litter?" the cat replied.

I needed to seek wisdom from my friend Ingrid. She knows everything there is to know about cats. She is a distressed cat magnet. I suspect her house is equipped with a radar that emits a kind of coded signals to distressed cats with a 50 miles radius, "distressed puss, come in, distressed puss, can you hear me, over".

"Ingrid, tell me about cat litter?" I was on the phone to my friend, the cat expert. She didn't disappoint. I learned enough about cat litter to last a life time.

"I get mine from Jolly's and I use catsan."

"Oh, do you now?"

"Not for myself, for Benson and Saffy." Benson and Saffy are not her children, they are her cats.

So off I went to Waitrose, our local supermarket, and came back with a 10 litre bag of light weight cat litter which is "very absorbent, helps to control odours". I bought it because I liked its logo. It was a small black cat with a white front. It looked like Joseph.

For the first few weeks we kept the kittens in the annexe, where we set up a temporary cat nursery, complete with toys, boxes and a climbing frame. They were so young, Rocco didn't even know how to eat solids. I put food down: Joseph got the idea pronto, and dug in. Rocco looked at it, looking interested. He walked round it, but did nothing. This happened twice more, he didn't eat a thing, and started looking thinner.

"He doesn't know how to eat," Chris said.

He picked up a bit of cat food on his little finger, and rubbed it on Rocco's nose. Rocco licked it off, looked surprised, then realised what it was, and got stuck into the rest of the food! By next mealtime he'd forgotten again, but after the second demo he never looked back.

The cat books say we must socialise kittens from a very young age or they will grow up not trusting humans. As it turned out they didn't need the therapy, I did. If I thought my cat phobia had been cured by Healey, I was wrong. It turned out my acquired immunity was specific to one cat only, Big H. I needed further therapy.

So this was how it went. Cat books under my arms, I went into the annexe every two hours during the day, to feed them, to show them that I was their food fairy and that they must treat me with the greatest respect. I told them if they behaved themselves and obeyed me, we would be a very happy cat family. Very often I invited Joan, my domestic goddess, to join me. We would have a cup of tea while I received my therapy. It helped with her there. Joan loves animals.

The cat books say I must handle them physically, so I made attempts to touch them with gloves on initially. I wasn't confident enough to just walk up to them and grab them. I didn't have to bother, they ignored me completely. It was only when they dropped off to sleep that I could touch them; and stroke them!

Two weeks later we decided to introduce Healey to the new-comers. Up till then we had kept the kittens secret from him, though he smelled a metaphorical rat, as he would sniff and scratch under the annexe door. When the big day came, I opened the annexe door for him. One look inside H decided it was not for him, and he went for a U turn.

"Wrong house!" he announced.

Too late; I had already shut the door behind him.

"Put them in a rubbish bag and give them to the dustmen!" H spat, hissed and growled. It didn't make the kittens disappear into thin air so he decided to make himself disappear. He went to hide under an armchair, to turn himself into a carpet, except that he hissed. They gave him a wide berth as they ran about playing and fighting, but obviously thought he was a bit odd, a bit funny in the head.

H was hostile towards the kittens for a few months, but gradually accepted them (a bit like me and him, I thought). His presence gave me support, however, feeble it was. I sat on the armchair with H underneath, and together we watched the amazing acrobatic show that the two tiny kittens delivered.

They demonstrated a range of talents. I watched as they climbed the wooden frame like monkeys, ran like racehorses, wrestled like sumo and jumped like kangaroos. They dangled from curtains and ceiling lights, trying to grab each others' tails, and when I threw a paper ball to Joseph, he made it the most wonderful toy. He grabbed it in mid air and kicked at it furiously with his hind legs, shredding it to pieces. All the time Rocco was trying to work out the quickest way to get to the top of the bookcase. When Joseph got bored with the paper he started to chase his own tail. He went round and round for hours, like a toy you wind up with a key, but what energy!

"He will never catch his own tail," I said to the cat under the chair.

"It is not the tail, it's the fun of going round and round it."

"How do you know?"

"All kittens do that."

"H, you are reminiscing!"

"I am doing no such thing, I am a cat. I don't live in the past."

Joseph was getting a bit too excited by his own tail, he ran faster and faster after it.

"Does he know that his tail is part of his body?" I asked H.

"Try treading on it, you'll find out!" H replied grumpily.

The two brothers continued to box, pounce and tumble over each other. They were having great fun and didn't bother with me or Healey. Then very suddenly they decided that they had had enough, and just dropped down on the carpet and went to sleep, SAS on top of philosopher. I stroked them. They felt soft and warm. I felt a gentle throbbing under my hand. They were both purring. In sleeping they had turned into two beautiful and contented fur balls, completely harmless.

I struggled on. Three weeks later they had their first vaccination, and then they could be let out to the garden. There they would learn to be professional cats. Then the fun began. The kittens were blessed; and I was hooked.

My heart was charmed, although my nerves were sending out red alert signals. They were so small but so scary, they were too cat-like, blue eyes smiling with evil intent, staring into mine.

11. Descendants of The Tiger.

Chris was in London for a couple of days. This was another winter evening when heaven was very angry. The horizontal rain was accompanied by a howling wind. I was watching television in the sitting room. I had fed the three cats early in the kitchen. They stayed in a bit. Then I opened the backdoor to let them out. Healey slipped out without a backward glance. The two kittens, then about eight months old, didn't want to have anything to do with the outside world which had turned very nasty. I had to throw them out. I couldn't cope with them on my own. My heart told me to let them stay; they were too small, they needed warmth and protection. My nerves argued with my heart and the nerves won. So out they had to go.

I heard crying and scratching. The noise didn't come from the television. I turned down the volume and listened. The crying became frantic and the scratching became more intense. It came from outside the front door. I went to investigate. I turned the outside light on and peeped through the tiny viewing window. I immediately ducked away. Too late, they had seen me.

"Help us, help!" I looked again. Joseph and Rocco were totally drenched and shaking uncontrollably in the wind and rain. They wore a trusting expression and their pleading eyes were begging me to save them, to let them inside. Their cries tugged on my heartstring. I watched them in silence. I couldn't stand it. My heart began to beat faster. I could feel the fear of cats surfacing. I had tried to fool myself that I was ready for this, but deep down inside, I knew I would never be.

I turned the outside light off and returned to the television. The crying continued. I turned the TV volume up to drown their cries. I couldn't settle. My heart and my nerves were having a battle with each other, again.

"Let them in. They are so tiny, they need protection. Have you no compassion," my heart screamed at me.

"Oh no, once you get them inside you will never get rid of them. Remember, you still fear cats," my nerves reminded me.

"The cold may kill them, they need shelter," my heart sighed.

"They will go to join H in the penthouse up in the garage. They'll be OK," my nerves reassured me. I cared for them out of responsibility but I didn't care about them. Chris wanted them in the first place. Where was he now when they needed him? I was tired and I was angry. All this cat business had to stop. They had to go, I couldn't cope anymore. I was totally pissed off. I felt like punching a hole in the wall. Suddenly it went very silent. The crying had stopped.

Slowly I got up from the armchair and followed my legs which were carrying me towards the backdoor. They told me my heart had won the battle. I put on my heavy duty raincoat and Wellington boots. I put a big scarf round my neck and with a big torch in my hand, I went out to look for Joseph and Rocco. A blast of freezing air greeted me when I opened the backdoor. The rain had eased and the wind had dropped a bit. The outside automatic lights came on. I went straight to the garage hoping to find them there. I tried to open its door. It refused to open, the dampness had caused it to expand and the double doors had stubbornly stuck together. It would require the strength of a 16 stone man to wrench it open. Since I don't weigh 16 stone and am not a man, I crouched down to the level of the cat flap, holding the flap open I shouted, "H, are the kids with you?" I called their names, I apologised, I promised I would never treat them this way again. There was not a meow from them. They might be somewhere else, I thought. I went looking for them in the garden. I turned on the torch once I was out of range of the automatic lights. In complete darkness the garden had assumed an air of mystery and menace. I had no appetite for ghosts and witches. All I wanted to do was to find the kittens. I walked round sending the beam of the torch into dark corners. I tried to imagine where I would hide if I were only 10 inches tall. I crouched under bushes and shrubs and I called their names. There was no sign of them. I was freezing. I walked back to the house. I realised I did care about them.

I felt deflated and I was worried about them. I did what I always do in this kind of situation; I put the whole thing out of my mind and go to bed, and I will myself to sleep by counting sheep. On this occasion it didn't work.

It was one of those nights when more thinking about sleep was done than actually sleeping. I fluffed the pillows, rolled over, arranged and rearranged the duvet. It was no use and I found my brain went into overdrive.

What was it like to be a vulnerable kitten, with a heartless and neurotic owner that it had been dealt? I had no idea. I could only imagine, though I did know what it is like to be a girl in a Chinese family of twelve, with a cruel and domineering father.

The kittens did not have any choice about their new circumstances. I took them away from their mother. They were in a new place, living with someone they hardly knew. I was the source of all the things they needed; shelter, food, water, companionship and care. It was up to me to bring everything together and create a home for them. Why was I rejecting them? Why was I doing to them what my father did to me when I was a child.

Taking on the two kittens had thrown up a lot of issues for me. The way I treated them had caused me to re-examine my childhood experience in the hands of a cruel father.

I know what it was like to be left outside, in the dark and cold, and hungry.

****

I thought back to the time when my father punished me and my twin sister. OK, we deserved to be punished, as we were both very bad at our school work, and selfish when we played with other children. We disobeyed him; we refused to be friendly with the five children he had with his concubine. Father glowered at us, threatened us, hurt us and beat us with his belt: we were terrified of him. Then one night he threw us out of the house without our dinner. I was too young to analyse behaviour in adults. I was a child with a child's understanding. But I was also a child in an unusual family with a father who didn't care much about me.

Something happened inside me the night my father threw me out of the house. I reached the first landmark in my life's journey. I realised I must not allow myself to be damaged by someone who had never loved me. To minimise the damage, I made a decision to be invisible in father's presence. I thought, "I've had enough of this, please God, let me grow up fast, let me get away from him one day." My twin was more radical. "Let's run away tonight!"

"No," I said, "father is the head of police, there is nowhere we can hide."

We stopped playing and started to study really hard, and I discovered the joy of books. That was the night that my brain woke up.

Eventually, we both got away, to England.

****

I rose very early the following morning and went straight to open the back door. From there I could see the garage door and the cat flap clearly. I shouted their names. I rang their food bowl with a fork, a signal that they had learned to mean food was being served. Moments later a black kitten with a white front and four tiny white paws dashed through the cat flap, followed by a black kitten with a tiny white bow tie, followed by H, the master himself. The two kittens ran towards me, laughing and shouting the whole way, with heads and tails in the air. They were so eager and pleased to see me, as if they had spent a night in Aladdin's Cave and they wanted to tell me all about it. They had jogged, shaved and showered and were now ready for a hearty breakfast of bacon, sausage and eggs.

"F-o-o-d!" Joseph shouted.

He was the first one to sit down at the breakfast table. I served them their order with fried toast thrown in. The kittens tucked in straight away.

"Oh, it is delicious, is there anymore?" Joseph enquired. I refilled his bowl twice. Joseph was the greediest of the three. He would go on to eat for Wales.

"What happened last night?" H gave me a long hard look.

"It's a long story, I'll tell you later."

For now I had wholeheartedly adopted Joseph and Rocco. I could always start being heartless again another day.

****

Exaggerating your own strength not only frightens your enemy,
It raises your fighting spirit too!

(Feng Menglong)

The kittens proved expert at exaggeration, demonstrating it brilliantly.

I watched the kittens grow and discovered a few fascinating truths about them.

They are born with an invisible battery that they hide about their person. When threatened, the battery switches itself on and the tiny fluffy kitten will immediately transform itself into a miniature incredible hulk: its eyes open wide to the size of ping pong balls, its paws turn into two pairs of high heel shoes, doubling its height, it arches its back and its fur stiffens to become a toilet brush. It walks differently too, sideway like a crab. It vibrates, turning itself into a live, high voltage wire! When the threat is over, the battery switches itself off and the vibrating toilet brush turns back into the exquisite kitten.

Kittens have great skills. They run, climb, box and kick like athletes, but without the years of training. They dangle from anything that hangs, like a trapeze artist. They shred net curtains, and your trousers or skirts, like a shredding machine. They are yoga experts and born contortionists, they twist and turn and squeeze into the most ridiculous space, and get themselves out again like Houdini. And they do all these at five weeks, with no training.

Their repertoire extends as they grow. At five months old they can jump a wall 6 feet high, from a standing jump in one go, no run up. They race up trees, leap from roof tops, jump into shrubs and bushes, burrow under leaves, attack anything that moves, all done with gusto. They catch a floating feather between their front paws while flying through the air. And as for fence-walking! Breathtaking: they stroll along it, sit down, doze in a most precarious poise, even U-turn on it. All done in the name of fun, but showing their illustrious ancestry. They are completely fearless.

I watched Rocco and Joseph perform these antics, apparently effortlessly. They fell and tumbled, picked themselves up, and seconds later started all over again. They self-taught, learning through play. They fell 10 times, and got up 11 times, getting better every time.

FREEDOM is built into their DNA: they instinctively reject being held tight or confined. DISOBEDIENCE is another part of their genetic make up, surfacing the minute they become independent. They go east when you want them to go west, and sleep in your shoe or on the bird table, in fact, anywhere, except the velvet cushion you offer them. They make their chosen bed the cosiest in the whole world, and they sleep like princes on their throne. Chris says they are not disobedient, of course, because they have no notion of any one else's desires, they do what they want. Sometime it coincides with what you want, sometimes not.

Kittens are fluffy fur missiles, they get everywhere. Their eyes are too big for their faces, their meows are too pathetic, their thundering purr out of proportion to their tiny throats, and they treat their tail and our arms and legs like toys. They behave in the most irresponsible and disrespectful manner.

Yet, they would grow up to survey the world coolly with the same big eyes; speak to the world with the same meow and purr, and the world succumbs. They walk tall, greeting the world with their tails straight up in the air. They walk into their home without asking for permission, come and go as they please, like spoilt princes. Who can blame them? After all, they are the descendants of the tiger.

No one can deny that kittens are the most divine creatures there ever have been. Only God can create such living beings who are completely fascinating, utterly compelling and totally fearless, yet compacted into a tiny fluffy body that can fit snugly into your hand. In time, they grow up and turn into graceful, mysterious beasts: cats, with a life and a story of their own.

Rocco and Joseph had completely won me over. The cat family was complete.

12. My Cats and I.

Befriend a virtuous person, you learn to be virtuous,
Befriend a witch, you learn witch craft,
Follow an evil man, you learn his evil way,
Follow a drifter, you drift away with him.

(Chinese proverb)

I would like to add: follow H and you learn to be a world class hunter.

"People are asking if I am their mother," Healey meowed at me. People were asking if I was their mother also.

"Are they your child-substitutes?" they enquired.

"What, do you think my cats look like me?" I said.

Over the years I have had a few comments about our childfree marriage.

"You have no children, no wonder Chris works so hard because you two have no family life," a relative sympathised, and of course she has children, not one, not two but a few.

"Have you tried adoption or IVF?" the wife of a judge I met at a wedding enquired. It was the first time we met. She went on to inform me that she has four children.

We would have liked to have children but it didn't happen. I do not crave for things that I do not have, I love and enjoy everything that I have now. This is a very valuable lesson I have learnt from my father at a very young age. The blessing in my marriage is that Chris feels the same way about life's gains and losses.

It may be true that some childfree women are consumed by regrets and a sense of failure. But how can you miss something that you've never had?

Perhaps my life would have been enriched by a family, but it hasn't happened. I have filled it with other things and I refuse to moan when I have so much to be grateful for. I walk this earth only once, every step is precious. I want to give life everything I am capable of. I don't want to ruin it by other women's opinion of my reproductive organs.

I don't even treat my three cats like kids. I am not a hard person, but I don't hold a misty-eyed view of parenthood. When asked why I haven't had children, I have the perfect answer, "The world is full of kids, if you want more you can have my quota."

****

The kittens were growing up fast. They had to learn to adapt to the great outdoors with all its surprises and dangers. Experience would come, but they must first learn the skills to master this jungle that we call the countryside. H had become their surrogate mother and teacher.

He didn't do the mothering bit very well; he never groomed, licked or washed them, but they followed him everywhere, often one on either side of him.

"They look more like his bodyguards than pupils," Chris observed. They learnt from H about hunting and survival, skills that their mother would have taught them, skills they would need to become professional cats. One sunny afternoon they were treated to a master class.

H was licking himself on a windowsill next to a gravel path. Across the path is a flower bed and lawn, edged by a low stone retaining wall. Joseph and Rocco were about six months old, play-fighting near the flower bed. Suddenly Joseph went into SAS mode, and started digging about by the bed. He was pawing at something.

"Don't try to hide, come out and fight like a man!" Joseph was shouting down a hole. Then he jumped back across the grass, holding in his mouth a small orangey-brown animal. It was bigger than a mouse, smaller than a rat, its furry tail as

long as its body and nearly as thick. Joseph had caught it, and ran a couple of yards with it wriggling in his mouth.

Then Joseph dropped it. He swiped at it with his paw, tried to grab it, slammed a paw flat down, and missed. The orange beast bit at Joseph's face, swung its claws, reared back, and swung again. A quarter of his size, it held Joseph off just as Joseph would have held off a dog, spitting and clawing. Then it darted towards its home. Halfway, it turned back at Joseph, spat and swung again. Joseph came on, but didn't come close. He knew enough to chase it, but not what to do next.

Rocco watched, ten feet away, interested, but not giving it much. Healey, though, was different. He stopped licking and raised his head, watching, still. Then he dropped silently from the windowsill, stalked across to the low wall, hopped onto it.

Joseph didn't notice, still focussed on his problem, not knowing how to crack it. Back and forth went the swiping and spitting, then the orange creature made a clean break towards its hole, running right across in front of H. H watched it come, then as it went by, made his move. Timing it exactly right, in one movement he whacked his paw down on the animal's back, pinning it; then he leant down, put his jaws round its neck and bit. Crunch: dead.

Then the Master turned, dropped back on the path and hopped back onto his windowsill. In a moment, he was asleep. That's the way to do it. Class dismissed.

> *An opportunity missed is lost forever,*
> *Success comes with seizing the moment.*
>
> (Feng Menglong)

****

Some people disapprove of cats killing wild life. Cat books and newspaper pet columns are full of advice for these people: fit a bell to their collars to warn prey of their presence, lock them up at night, de-claw them. One minute pussies are praised for catching rats and mice in the house, the next minute they are criticised and punished for catching birds and butterflies in the garden. What a confusing world we live in.

Wild cats hunt for food, to feed themselves and their offspring: they kill for survival. Domestic cats hunt, not necessarily for food, but to respond to their instinctual drives, or for fun and games, depending on how you see it. Wild or tame, their hunting skills are vital to their survival, and as long as they can hunt and kill they are independent. Hunting and sex are cat's basic instincts. We have chosen to neuter our cats to make them less likely to fight and spray, not to interfere with their sex life.

Human beings are programmed to eat and have sex, not to hunt. Cavemen had to hunt all those years ago for the same reason as the wild cats. Things are different now; we have places called supermarkets. We no longer need to hunt to survive. Yet we hunt for fun in the name of sport and competition. We are the most powerful and merciless predators on this planet, we hunt and we drive some species to extinction. Some people inflict great suffering on some of the most vulnerable creatures on earth. Some of these people can be the ones that put bells on their pussies. What a world we live in. I believe we are in no position to criticise our cats for catching the odd bird until we put our own house in order. Cats are probably the only domestic animal that is feted and hated at the same time.

To hunt or not, we have a choice, cats don't. They behave instinctively, their nature shouldn't be smothered. How would we feel if someone comes along to put a bell on us, or take measures to eradicate our eating and sex drives?

H continued to teach diligently by example, and the young cats continued to learn and practise enthusiastically. When Joseph and Rocco graduated to become world class hunters, H took early retirement.

****

Joseph loves his food. He waits by his food bowl in excitement at meal time, very often before time, and more often after it as well. He always demands more. He would come round to where I am and look up at me hungrily and adoringly. He says "Thank you" in a continuing thunderous purr while he eats, his whole body vibrates with pleasure. Healey and Rocco ate quietly and often looked up at me as if to say, "are you giving him LSD again?"

Joseph took advantage of H at meal time. When he finished his own food he would dive straight into Healey's food bowl and gulp down whatever was there. H would stand and stare into space, he didn't fight, didn't growl, he just let Joseph take his food. This reminded me of the way he was left out when he was fed alongside his family by his previous owner. His childhood experience still haunted him. I felt it my duty to enforce his position as senior cat and protect him from bullying by a young thug like Joseph. I often had to push Joseph away so that H could finish his food. When they went to the cattery I told the owners to feed H separately, away from Joseph, the only bully among our three cats, so I thought. I was very wrong.

One morning I had decided to work in the dining room. I paint in my studio but I often write in other rooms, just to have a change of scenery. And the scenery before me couldn't be more friendly and cordial. H and Rocco were sleeping under the radiator. Joseph was sleeping in his basket, also under the radiator but about 2 feet away from H.

I was editing a chapter for the third time on my laptop. A passage made me laugh out loud, for the third time. I took one big breath, highlighted the passage, and hit the "delete" button on the computer. One week's work disappeared instantly. A multi-millionaire best selling novelist, whose name I cannot remember, once said, "If you laugh or cry over your own words, get rid of them, kill them. It is self indulgence, it is not good writing." I have no way of finding out whether or not this is good practice, but you cannot ignore the advice from someone who has made millions from his books.

Having killed my own words I looked up and noticed the peaceful scene had moved down one notch. H was now standing in front of Joseph. He had his back to me so I couldn't see his face. Joseph was half sitting and half leaning on the side of the basket, his face turned to one side and his eyes dipped. I looked on in surprise as H lifted his right paw and started to beat up Joseph. The blows came hard and fast. He was beating Joseph's left ear into submission. Joseph bowed his head and made no move to fight back. Rocco looked on. He didn't record the assault on his mobile phone but was watching H's every move. Sometimes Rocco's non-involvement tactic concerned me. He was just a little bit too philosophical for a young cat.

I was shocked. I shouted at H to stop. He had chosen to be deaf, for the beating continued. Had this happened before? I had never thought that H was capable of violence. Battle for dominance is nature to all species, animals and humans; in the jungle, within a family unit, in school playgrounds. I don't intentionally mix with people who are looking for a fight, so I do not really understand what drives them. A social study shows that victims of domestic violence often go to the police after an average of 30 assaults by their partners or spouses. Well, I still have the whole 30 to go.

I went over. "What is going on?" I asked.

"*H is beating up JJ, he has done nothing wrong,*" Rocco explained. JJ is Joseph's pet name.

"I can see that," I said. But I also saw that H had no intention of hurting the young cat. His claws were sheathed. He was asserting his authority, to put this young thug in his place. He had chosen a moment when Joseph was fast asleep, in his own basket, under a warm radiator and in my presence. In other words he caught Joseph totally off guard. I know this well. I am the second youngest in a family of seven. Younger siblings are a nuisance; they need to be put in their place every now and then by the older brothers or sisters. Timing is vital. The big one will choose the moment when the young one is totally off guard; to pull a hair, and to pinch a bottom.

"H, stop being so silly," I said. I am a self respecting individual. It would be beneath my dignity to threaten or intimidate anyone, so I decided to reason with my cat.

"If you don't stop immediately I'll break your neck." Reasoning worked. H stopped. He looked at me with utter disdain, as if to say, "*what? Me, I wasn't even there.*" He walked away, back to his favourite spot under the radiator, to read the carpet.

"JJ, are you OK?" I stroked him.

"*No, it hurts.*"

"Where does it hurt?"

"*My paws hurt, my tummy and my tail also hurt,*" he said enthusiastically.

Apparently it hurt everywhere. And he still managed to get up and limped feebly towards his food bowl.

"*F-o-o-d!*" he cried.

Healey sulked after the scolding. He stayed away from me for hours, "*You are not worth it,*" his big round eyes told me. And I thought I read him like a book.

Was H resentful of the affection that I showered on the two young cats?

I now lived with three cats. They became my constant companions as I worked at home. They were funny and entertaining and they made me laugh a lot with their playful antics and games with each other. They don't do overt affection like kissing or putting a paw round you when you need a helping hand. For me a soft purr and a meow was enough.

I kept up on the latest recommendations on cat care. I had assumed that my cats were happy with three activities: stuffing their faces on demand, lying belly up in the sun when weather permitted, and sleeping for hours on end by a hot radiator. I was wrong. According to cat experts I must have regular playtime with them, particularly the two young ones. Lack of regular human contact could turn them into psycho cats.

I set about to train them to play with me. This proved to be more difficult than I had thought. I was still very nervous with them. Any toys and games that required close contact with cats would trigger my dormant phobic trait. I had to play with them at arm's length with a remote control device

Plan A was a stuffed mouse with a very long tail, which I bought in the local pet shop. I spotted a good moment to start the play therapy. I found all three cats sleeping in the sitting room. I sat near them with a big grin on my face, "boys, see what I have got you!" I tickled their noses with the mouse tail. Healey scratched his nose with his eyes shut, Joseph sat up, stretched and yawned, well, at least he woke up. Rocco looked at H who was now awake. He gave junior an *"I have no idea what it is all about, but just ignore her and she will go away"* look. I tried again and again. Several minutes later I gave up when they all dispersed.

Out came plan B: two jingle balls which I bought from the same shop. The packaging said the game is great fun for cat and human and it guarantees instant bonding between the two. I rolled the balls on the carpet at their direction. To encourage their full co-operation I sang to the jingle of the balls. Joseph responded enthusiastically for about 30 seconds, then he got bored. Healey and Rocco hid under the sofa and refused to have anything to do with plan B. I exercised extreme patience. I threw the balls at them, no one moved. I ran to retrieve them myself, rolled them again and retrieved them again. I became the sole player in this game. After ten rounds I'd had enough. I stretched out on the carpet and looked around, the cats were gone.

13. A Mother's Love.

Before Healey I had wanted a dog or three. I had fond memories of my childhood dog Lucky, who lived to the grand age of sixteen.

Chris dislikes dogs. Early on in our married life I had tried to influence him into getting a dog. I was in a strong position then, I could play the new wife card. Surely a loving husband would do anything to please his new wife. I had it all worked out. I would take care of all the practical side of things. I would do all the toilet training, clean up immediately after any accidents, no complaints, no shouting at dog or man. I would do all the shopping for the dog: food, basket, collar and blanket. I would look for a kennel for when we went on holiday. I would walk him twice daily, this would apply to all weather. Chris did not have to lift one finger in his care, except to pay all the vet, kennel and food bills. The division of responsibility couldn't be fairer. The new wife card didn't work. So I played the lonely wife card. "I am always alone, a dog will protect me and keep me company when you are away." I said to him many times, accompanying my plea with sighs and wearing my best lonely heart expression. "Stop being so creepy!" he cried out loud.

Eventually I decided to end the campaign. It would be unkind to bring a dog into a home where half the population ignores him, disregards him, and would have nothing to do with him.

While the two young cats were lively, full of tricks and frequently hilarious to watch, it was H who was with me all the time. He would wander off briefly to do what a cat had to do and then he would return to sit somewhere where he could follow me with his eyes. He listened to me and never said a word. He gave no advice, no criticism like a friend would do. He seemed to know when I was happy, sad, or just needed a quiet moment all by myself, and with him. I knew he loved me and I knew he knew he had made me love him.

Healey had lived through a few significant events: the return of Hong Kong from the United Kingdom to the People's Republic of China on 1st July 1997. This marked the end of British rule and the transfer of sovereignty of Hong Kong to China; he saw in the millennium with us; the 11th September 2001 terrorist bombing of the Twin Towers of the World Trade centre in New York City; the deaths of my mother-in-law in 1999; and the death of my friend Ingrid's mother in 2003. More significantly he was with me when I received the news that my mother had passed away. How I still remember that day!

It was 8.15 in the morning of 13th June 2000. Chris had already left for work. I had just come in from the garden when the telephone rang. It was my brother Ki Shun. He told me mother had walked away from us all a couple of hours ago. He had just returned home from the hospital where she died. There was a lot to do and he would get back in touch once the funeral arrangements were made. We were both very calm.

For many years mother had lived with Ki Shun and his family. When she started to require regular nursing assistant, she was moved to a nursing home in the north of Hong Kong island. She had been there for a few years now. She was far from happy with the arrangement, "What is the point of having children! They shut you out and dump you in a tip like this when you are old and defenceless. Your father would never allow this to happen to me," she said to me every time I visited her.

Chris and I had been back in Hong Kong five months earlier. We visited her in the old people's home every day. She seemed fine but had not been feeling too good. After we left her health deteriorated and was taken to hospital three weeks before. She didn't improve. The news was not unexpected. She died on her 88th birthday. She left behind seven children, ten grandchildren and eight great grandchildren. Five of her children were by her bedside when she took her last breath. Some Chinese would call this a life fulfilled.

It was a sunny and warm day. I got myself a cup of tea and went out to sit in the garden under the blooming wisteria. Healey jumped up on the bench, curled up beside me and sat there staring into space. Over in the field Joseph was stalking a poor soul. Both Chris and I are keen gardeners. He deals with the heavy tasks like digging, mowing, pruning, composting and tending the vegetable patch. I deal with the demanding areas of flowers and green house stuff, both require tender loving care and constant attention, the kind of tasks that suit me very well. I looked around me and saw all sorts of flowers in bloom, roses, tree peony, poppies, alyssum, lilies, jasmine, honeysuckle and many more, except gladioli. My mother loved gladioli. She loved their tall and upright stalks and bold and bright flowers. She always had a big display of gladioli at home. I had tried growing them in the garden without success. Suddenly I had this urge to see gladioli. I got back into the house, grabbed the car keys, drove to the nearby flower shop and got myself half a dozen gladioli, ones with loud bright red flowers, just how my mother liked them. Once home I arranged them in a big vase on the window sill and lit a candle in front of it. I sat on the floor looking at the display.

My mother had just died and I should be howling with grief and loss, instead I went to buy flowers. Why wasn't I crying? Had I no feelings for her? It was abnormal behaviour. I tensed up and willed myself to cry. There was no tear. Someone in a black fur coat walked in. In a warm day like this I did not understand why he kept his fur coat on. Healey came up to me, nudged me with his head and sat down right next to me. He purred his quiet purr. I stroked him. His fur felt so smooth and silky and comforting. He had kept his thick fur on for me. He carried on purring and I could feel the vibrations in his neck. Slowly I relaxed and I smiled at the gladioli, they seemed to smile back at me .The thought of my mother has always brought a smile to my face. Her memory has this effect on me. Unlike the flowers she loved, my mother was no beauty and at four feet two inches tall, she cut a small figure with a rotund belly, which she said was due to bearing the seven of us. What she lacked in stature and looks she made up for by her genes. Mother had to have unusual genes to live through what she had gone through. I believe her life story warrants a book by itself.

****

My mother was illiterate. She never went to school and couldn't read or write. She married a tough, driven and domineering man who was my father. For almost all of her married life she was made to accept his concubine and her five children by him.

Keeping a concubine was not uncommon among Chinese men of my father's generation. Concubines are the men's appendage and are usually given inferior status as subordinate of the legally married wife. My father put her up in a flat about 10 miles from our own home.

He had established this woman as my mother's equal and treated her five children with overt affection and attention. He had undermined my mother's position as the legally married wife. His behaviour was humiliating to her to the extreme and caused her immense grief. My mother had no "revenge" genes in her. She wouldn't know what to do with revenge even if she had it. Neither did she have the strength nor brain to manipulate her fate, so I had thought. I was to prove myself very wrong! She tolerated father's other woman, swallowed all the humiliations and dealt with the situation in a silent and dignified manner. She yielded to him completely and unconditionally. Against all odds she brought up seven of us, her own children. She lived to survive the marriage and him.

When I was older I understood why mother always looked subdued, with great sadness in her eyes. He set all the rules and expected his two women and twelve children to live by them.

Father was educated, intelligent and hard working. He had a strong desire to succeed and a great sense of responsibility. These attributes enabled him to get to the very top of his chosen career path. By the age of 35 he held a high ranking post in the uniformed division of The Royal Hong Kong Police Force, the first Chinese appointed to that position. At the time Hong Kong was a British colony, all top Government jobs were given to British and Irish expatriates. The Chinese had to be exceptional to get noticed for promotion.

Mother bravely kept up a cheerful front with us children and never attacked father in our presence. Many years later during one of my visits back home I asked her if she had ever thought of walking out on him. He had died a few years previously. And you know what, she gave me an hour's lecture in his defence, which summed up like this, "Are you kidding, walk out with seven tiger cubs on tow, all with fiery temper and insatiable hunger. How on earth can I fill seven rice bowls? Your father could have walked out on us and he didn't. He worked hard to feed and educate the tiger cubs. We were never short of anything. It is most ungrateful of you to suggest that I should have walked out on him!" She went on to say, "The day your father brought that wretched woman home was the most miserable day of my life. I would walk out if I was on my own. I would fill my rice bowl working as a domestic maid, or may be, a dim sum waitress in a tea house."

"Mother, I would go for the tea house job if I were you, there you can eat dim sum all the time." Mother laughed.

****

It wasn't laughing matter. I saw the light. All these years my mother had lived for one thing: to keep her seven children together. She didn't make waves or rock the boat so that we were properly provided for and were given a proper education. She had found her happiness nurturing us and watching us grow. It was strength. We didn't disappoint her. We have all grown up to be decent, responsible and honest individuals. She has demonstrated to me that happiness is in loving and nurturing what you have, and not to crave for what you have not.

I have always known that she had never wanted me and my twin sister to leave home. She thought she understood why we left; to escape father. I told her that it was not the only reason. I left home voluntarily to learn to be independent and to make a life for myself. I knew she had never accepted this. I had promised her that I would return home when I had achieved what I set out to achieve. That didn't happen. Years on I am still living and working in a foreign land, away from all my family, all for the love of one man.

My twin sister had vowed never to return home once she got out. Decades later she is back there, living alone. She sees selected members of our large extended family once or twice a year, and abstains from all family gatherings. Sadly mother had gone when she returned home to settle. Fate has treated me and my twin sister very differently. Sadly over the years we have drifted apart emotionally, but one thing remains between us: our love for our mother.

****

Healey stirred beside me. "Grandmother has walked away from us." I said to him. He gave me his trademark soulful look as if he understood. He then got up and made his way towards his feeding station in the kitchen. I fed him. I returned to sit by the vase of gladioli and I broke down completely.

14. Home Life.

The greatest blessing comes from a simple life,
The greatest happiness comes from contentment.

(Anon)

Healey and Rocco regarded Joseph as a younger brother that they could do without but would tolerate. Joseph was in awe of Healey. While he would mess about with Rocco, he was always at his best behaviour towards the senior cat.

"Why does H look at me in such a funny way?" Joseph purred at me. I looked at Healey.

"That funny way is what we Chinese call an inscrutable look."

"What does that mean?"

"It means he knows everything about you, and you know nothing about him," I explained.

"Wow, that is scary!"

"Quite!"

When H realised that I wasn't going to give the kittens to the dustmen, he accepted them into his big heart. With them he was gracious but serious, firm but not fierce, cool but not distant. While they ran riot with the birds and leaves in the garden, he would meditate or snooze in the shade. The three cats seemed to know what the Chinese know:

To show respect for your seniors is to observe the etiquette of
rank and age;
To regard your juniors with consideration is to honour talents
and good behaviour.

(Mencius)

We decided to have the kittens neutered. When we went to fetch them from the vet after the operation, Joseph spat at Chris, *"you bastard!"* he hissed. Rocco sat in the basket

76

contemplating life as an asexual creature. We might have modified their hormones, but we couldn't alter the wild blood in them.

Joseph and Rocco were like the strong wind in autumn, wherever they went they blew leaves off the trees. Compared to their youthfulness and energy, H appeared slow and reserved, like an old sage, not interested in anything. He had seen it all, done it all.

His quiet self confidence made him almost invisible and he had this way of moving silently beneath everyone's notice. His inscrutability and calm confidence was so huge that no one, humans or cats, questioned his status. He never had to prove a thing. But like some truly great, unforgettable leaders of the world, H had a steely resolve.

Chris was beginning to find him a bit boring. I held a different view. Healey was like a mountain, solid and dull from afar, get closer and one would discover all the hidden surprises and beauties. His reserved and laid back behaviour hid great strengths and wisdom. He was modelling himself more and more on the reclusive life style of ancient Chinese sages. When he'd had enough he would seek me out, park himself close to me and be aloof.

H helped to bring up the kittens, and was generous in his teaching. H wouldn't permit the kittens to be just ordinary hunters, and the brothers didn't disappoint. Between the three, they kept the rabbits down. Chris's plan had worked. He said we should have another three cats so that there was someone on duty in the vineyard at all times. I told him if he was not careful I might put HIM out there at all times! He smiled.

We were beginning to see the fruits of our endeavour since we moved to Wales. The work in the garden, the vineyard and the greenhouse took up a lot of our spare time. There were defeats and victories, and we became wiser with each set back and success. The two kittens thrived in this environment. Initially, I was nervous about letting them out at night with all the dangers of cars and larger predators in the dark. They might get mugged or beaten up by feral youths who roam the street looking for happy slap fun. I had wanted to lock them up at night. I was concerned about the down side of this free come-and-go as you like life-style. Chris's view is that a free cat is a happy cat. He believes the extra happiness is worth the risk.

"Cats are programmed to roam and hunt at night. You have to let them go."

Chris always speaks up for them. Sometimes I felt I had FOUR cats.

Healey remained my constant companion. His happiness and contentment were infectious. When I felt unhappy, the sight of this magnificent cat would always make me smile. The two kittens and H had gradually moved from being strangers into settled companionship. They seemed happy and contented. I, too, had settled and had learnt to embrace, and love, life on this hillside.

This corner of Wales is unique. The land is made up mainly of gentle hills, green valleys, woods, rivers, canals, meadows and huge rainbows. They support a wide range of wildlife, farm animals, birds and fish. In the hills and valleys farms and houses dotted around. In spite of what the politicians say about the economy, a few market towns are still thriving. This is a place where people work with nature and respect the land.

This place is perfect for walking. In a single day you can climb hills, cross a flowing stream on stepping stones and cross a canal over ancient bridges, with grazing sheep for company. We have walked most of the nearby footpaths along the Welsh borders, sometimes just the two of us, sometimes with friends and relatives. We have learnt to cater for the Welsh weather. We can set out in bright sunlight and get caught in torrential rain or hailstorm later.

Over the years Chris and I have travelled the world, but are always pleased to come home to Wales. We entertain and are entertained, but love best the quiet weekends and cosy evenings at home. We make time for things that really matter to us both. There is nothing we like better than to cook a nice three course meal, take our time over dinner and chat over a glass or three of wine. We call this togetherness. When I cook I do the washing up. When Chris cooks, which is often, I also do the washing up, sometimes I also wash the floor, depending on how he cooks what he cooks. Occasionally he washes up and puts the pots and pans on the draining board to dry. When he leaves the kitchen I will take them off the draining board, wash them again, dry them with a hand towel and put them back in the cupboard. No moans, no arguments. We both accept that division of labour is all part of togetherness.

You don't really know what a person is like until you live with them, and to experience at first hand their virtues and weaknesses. Chris is a very patient teacher. It took him six months to teach me the basic computing and email skills. It took another six months for me to become competent in both, requiring a lot of trouble shooting from him in the process. I don't do Facebook, I don't twitter, and I don't do webcam, simply because it will take him a life time to teach me. And it will take me another life time to learn it. He will have the patience to teach me. I do not have the patience nor the inclination to learn this. I already live a full life.

Chris is good at problem solving. I am good at creating problems. "I am a doctor, doctors are trained to solve problems," he often says. He is persistent and focused. I am an expert at switching focus and he calls it giving up too easily. He discusses one thing at a time. I comment on 5 or 6 topics in one conversation. He does one thing at a time. Like most women I am a multi task genius. I can feed the cats, empty the washing machine, and at the same time talk on the phone to my brother in Hong Kong. I do all the pleasant things to our cats; like feeding them and spoiling them. He does all the unpleasant things like giving them injections and tablets. He calms me down when I get over excited about life's little surprises, or sad about its little setbacks. In return I often make him laugh with my own version of English.

"It is wet out there, I need to put on my Wellington," I would say.

"The left or the right one?" Chris would ask.

"Look, this scene is straight out of a Western spaghetti," I would say.

"Or maybe a spaghetti Western," he would reply.

"Gail is like a mother earth to her ponies," I would say.

"In English we call it earth-mother," he would say.

"The driver in that red car is so rude, I feel like putting up three fingers to him."

"Well, we do two fingers in this country. But by all means raise an extra finger if you want to register your disgust in your special Chinese way," Chris would laugh.

Doctors are not meant to treat their families, and Chris never doctors me.

"Chris, I think I have a tooth abscess."

"Go to see your dentist," he replied.

"Chris, I am seeing light flashes."

"Go to see your optician," he replied.

"Chris, there is a funny sensation in my tummy, I am worried."

"Go to see your doctor," he replied.

"What if I need surgery?"

"We can probably manage a colostomy between us," he replied.

"Chris, I think Joseph has an abscess in his forehead." He didn't reply, but within minutes Joseph was sitting on his lap, having his whiskers rubbed, his ears stroked, and his abscess palpated by a pair of large and skilled hands. He never does that to me.

The cats liked to chill out with us in the evenings. Joseph would lounge on Chris's ample stomach and Rocco would settle on his generous lap. The three of them would watch Master Chef or Dr Who on television, depending on who was in charge of the remote control. Healey would take up his usual position under the radiator where he would doze. Occasionally he would look up to check that I was still in sight. Healey would prefer to sit on my lap. I don't do lap top cats, my nerves would not allow me. The cats knew it.

Then Joseph would get bored and would knead and pound the man's stomach into submission before settling down to a deep sleep. Rocco would sink into the man's lap and before long he would start snoring. I didn't do any of that to Chris. I just settled into my favourite armchair with a book. Before long I would also fall asleep. We had a word for this; we called it togetherness. We live a semi reclusive life and we love it. But life could be mysterious and full of surprises, because unknown to us, trouble was already brewing in the mind of one of our cats. A misfortune was waiting round the corner.

****

There is a very old Chinese saying on freedom:

Gold is precious, love ranks even higher;
But for the sake of freedom I will forsake them both.

Freedom is precious to all creatures great and small, not just to human beings.

Joseph's life would be perfect if it were not for the necessary trips to the vets and the cattery. He has done these trips many times now, but he still hates the cat basket.

Cat books tell you how to do everything. However, like the instructions on a flea powder spray we tried out ("spray the animal all over, then allow the animal to stand for twenty minutes": allow it to stand? It was all we could do to keep it in the room!), they are sometimes somewhat optimistic. On the subject of car trips with cats, one cat book says: "Open the basket door and invite your cat to go inside. Failing that, hold it by the scruff of its neck, gently push it inside the basket and close the door. Both you and your cat will purr all the way to the vet." It is never like that in my house.

"Hold the basket still and stop panicking!" 'The man who understands cats' growls at me, whenever we want to get the cats inside.

I would steady one basket, and quick as lightning, Chris would grab Healey first and drop him into it, head on. "One down, two to go." By then the two juniors were going round and round in circles, hiding under chairs and behind cupboards, in an attempt to escape a fate they believed to be worse than death. Rocco would put up feeble resistance, but would be imprisoned within seconds. Two down, one to go.

"What are you doing! Put me down immediately!" the SAS cat hissed at Man.

"Come on Joseph, it is only a basket, you know it well," Man said assertively.

"NO! You like it so much, you get inside!"

At this point Cat promptly turned himself into a slippery eel. Man grabbed Cat. Cat wriggled and slipped away. Man and Cat went round and round in circle. Man got impatient and tried to pull Cat out from under the table. SAS Cat protested and lashed out. I saw blood.

"Shall I fetch you your gardening gloves, the one made of real leather," I enquired.

"Don't be so silly, who needs boxing gloves, I have claws," Cat shouted at me.

"Don't be so silly, now hold the basket up, be firm!" Man shouted at me. This was far too exciting for all of us.

There was more blood. Man swore for England. Cat swore for England, Wales and China! He had learnt the F word from a TV chef. My Welsh brother-in-law Dai Tom taught him the Welsh word for XX?*******X. I was quite startled by this turn of events. Stunning, I thought, this splendid young cat was learning languages! Just think of that. But who had taught him the Chinese swear word [^^]!ZZ!Y{@@}? I certainly didn't.

Eventually Man won and Cat was locked up in the basket.

"I thought you were on my side. I never thought you would sink so low," Joseph hissed at me while Chris put a band aid strip on his wound.

"Sorry JJ, but this has to be done."

"You wait! I know where you live."

Once in the car the real pantomime began. Joseph wailed and screamed through the air holes in the basket, informing the world that he had been KIDNAPPED and would someone please alert the police IMMEDIATELY.

"JJ, be quiet. You are just going for an injection in the vet's, you know all of them, they won't hurt you," I tried to calm him down.

"Now they threaten to DRUG me. Will someone please tell my mother to pay the ransom IMMEDIATELY."

This pantomime repeated itself every time in a car trip. Rocco and Healey had no appetite for this. They sat in their basket quietly. Healey would read The Daily Telegraph that I used to line the basket. It would be beneath his dignity to complain or resist. Rocco would contemplate life in captivity. Joseph would plumb new depths of emotion at each journey: *WOO, EEE, EURGH* do not begin to do justice to his sound effects, you would need a musical score as well to get the full feel of it.

The carrier basket seems to be synonymous with imprisonment and loss of freedom to the cats. I wouldn't like to be put inside a basket and be carried about to where I know not, and I am not even a cat. I understand my cats' fears. I wish I had a magic wand that would enable me to beam them (and me and Chris) to the vet. It would save a lot of anxiety; and blood.

15. Stars.

Life in rural Wales has not changed me, in that I am the same person as when I was living in the big cities. But my attitudes have changed. In the cities I had ambitions, here I have aspirations. There I had drive, needing to be on top of things, here I take things easy, occasionally allowing things to get on top of me. There life was a treadmill, here I can do what I like and when I like. Here the massive space, the silence and strangely the lack of sensory over-stimulation brings calmness to life. An added bonus is the absence of incessant unavoidable human contact. I have learned to value these aspects of country life and I no longer crave for the city. Chris and I are not great party animals. We prefer gardening and walking. We have both developed interesting pastimes and remain interested in the things we love doing. What we both miss are proper Chinese and Indian restaurants where we can get proper and carefully prepared ethnic food.

We are able to see more of Chris's family. When his parents were alive we made a point of visiting them in West Wales at least once a month. We continued to visit Pa after my mother-in-law died. I also got to know Chris's siblings and their families a lot better. With them I am able to share some of the fun and support that only amicable siblings can give one another.

People are often thrown together in a mysterious way. Many would make connection and go on to make an impact on one another's lives, like your neighbours, colleagues, your doctor and dentist, your hairdresser and your local library assistant. You are glad to see these people. You chat, not to delve into people's secrets, just to catch up, to gossip a bit, to trade stories on births, deaths, anniversaries, success and failures. Things like these bond and connect people.

Over the years I have crossed path with a number of people, some are memorable, others very forgettable. I view the bad one as meteors. They come from nowhere, stay in your radar very briefly and disappear without trace, hopefully forever. The good people are stars, they bring light and joy. The really good ones make a difference to your life and they are not replaceable. Here are a few stars that I have met on this Welsh hillside.

****

Shortly after moving to Wales I began to look for someone to help me with house work. I asked around.

"Good and reliable domestic helpers are like gold dust here," everyone told me. Those who had one guarded her like gold; she was not to be poached. I almost gave up when fate intervened. The gold dust came disguised as Joan Harland.

At the time Joan was newly widowed and was seeking part time work to give herself a reason to get out of bed in the morning. A mutual acquaintance put her on to me. One May morning she came to view the job.

"My daughter and son-in-law live in a house this size," she said as I showed her round.

"Do I call you and your husband Mrs and Dr H?" she asked as I poured her a cup of tea.

"Oh no, first names will do," I replied.

"I am viewing another job later today, I'll let you know my decision this evening."

That evening she called. I got the job. It was fifteen years ago. Joan is now our domestic goddess, occasional cat sitter and house key holder. She has become a trusted and firm friend. We spend many happy tea breaks in the kitchen, chatting about life and changing the world, kinds of things that women enjoy doing. Joan is fully engaged with life. She is always busy with her two children, four grandchildren and two great grandchildren. In her spare time she goes cruising (on cruise ships!) and dancing. In spite of leading such a full life she still finds time to spoil her dog and cat, Chloe and Oscar, rotten. When she needs time off she comes to help me with house work.

"Has Joan been?" Chris asked.

"Yes, and why?" I said.

"She has moved my papers, I can't find the one I am working on. Tell her to leave my papers alone," Chris said.

"Tell Chris I never move his papers. I take them up, dust underneath and put them back on the spot," Joan said.

"Explain to her that no dust can collect underneath papers, there is no need to dust underneath them," Chris said.

The cats loved Joan but hated it when she waved the Hoover about. Joan has this way of moving the Hoover about like a sub machine gun. As soon as she came round with it, Healey and Rocco would dash out of the cat flap immediately, one at a time. Joseph would sit in his basket and stare menacingly at Joan, refusing to move. I often watch as Joan smooth talks Joseph, "Come on JJ, time you got up."

The cat would remain silent and motionless. Joan would switch off her weapon, pick up the basket with the cat in it and put it down gently in a different spot. Then she would Hoover the spot where the basket was. When she finishes she would reverse the act and JJ would be under the radiator again. All the time she talks to the cat, and the cat just glowers at her.

"There is no need to clean under my bed, it is SO unnecessary," Joseph would come up to me after Joan leaves.

"Why not?" I stroke him.

"Dust cannot gather underneath my bed."

"JJ, be fair, you wear a fur coat and you like to play hide and seek under your bed. Joan is kind to you. I would throw you out myself," I would reason with him.

"You are a hard one," Joseph always has the last word, like his master.

We have this conversation every time after Joan has been. I have no issues with Joan's housekeeping methods and standards. The house feels so fresh and clean after she has been. I just go round moving the sofas back to where I want them. When Chris comes home he would also go round, moving the sofas back to where he wants them.

Chris and Joan get on famously. Every woman needs a woman like Joan round the house. And I am guarding her like gold dust.

****

Ruth lived in the farm house across the courtyard from us. She was a very good neighbour and over the years we have become firm friends. She came into our life with a big package: her daughter Mabel whom we watched grow up; her son Duncan who trained as a lawyer but is now working in the family firm. Her team of staff. And her cats; Joshua, Coco, Lily, and dogs; Max and Bella, and the horses. Sadly the whole family moved to live and work abroad over a year ago. I no longer have a companion with whom, in Chris's absence, I can share a home cooked Chinese meal and a bottle of wine while we talk late into the night. It takes someone special to do that with.

****

The Cottage sits on the edge of the canal bridge, midway between the bottom of the lane and our house. It used to belong to an old man, when he died it was left to his relatives. The cottage stayed unoccupied for a few years until Gail and Rob moved in. They transform the atmosphere of the lane immediately, forever. They bring colours and life to it. In spring and summer the front garden is a riot of flowers and plants. It brings a smile to my face whenever I drive past it. More often than not Rob is seen sitting in his deck chair, smiling and waving as neighbours pass by in their cars.

"He talks to everyone, people think that he is the village idiot," Gail said to me, rolling her eyes to heaven. Well, this village idiot has a Master's Degree in Environmental and Conservation Studies. He is also the secretary of the local conservation group. Rob is often seen clearing snow and gritting the lane on snowy days. He helps dig cars out when they are stuck in the snow. Chris has been at the receiving end of his kindness. I can't remember ever seeing Rob without a smile on his face. The world can do with more village idiots like him.

"He has a degree in conservation and I am the one who goes round switching lights off after him and turning down the central heating," Gail told me over the garden fence. I know what she means and I empathise.

Gail is slim. She has a tough face and there is a sparkle in her watchful eyes that tell people not to mess with her. I suppose you need to look tough when you are the manager of a local government office, dealing with problem public and red tape. The same face and eyes would break into an infectious laugh when we joke with each other. Gail and I indulge in sharing news. Some people may call it gossiping, but I call it keeping up to date with your neighbour. She, like me, adopts the rural dress code while at home; old jumpers, preferably ones with a few holes in the sleeves, and old trousers. Gail always dresses smartly when she goes to work. I often dress in Chris's cast offs when I work. My favourites are his winter cast-offs collection: big fleece lined wool shirt which I wear as a maxi shirt. They are so big on me that I can fit in two or three more layers underneath. Most fashion-minded women start with a pair of tight thigh high boots and work up from there. I start with a maxi shirt and work down from there, no tight boots, just baggy trousers and thick socks. I don't wear them to recycle or to save the world. It is about freedom and the confidence to wear what is comfortable and not be bothered by the mismatch or fashion.

Gail and Rob rescue abused Shetland ponies and care for them in their field. We have some spare land at the top of our field and have invited them to put their ponies there when their own field needs time to recover. There are four Shetland ponies; Billy, Zac, Thomas and Diddy. These four beautiful creatures have grown on me and I have offered to be their official godmother. Gail and Rob hold their charge in high regard and fondness. They come up to see them twice a day, in all weather, to stroke them and talk to them. I too, stroke and talk to them (the ponies). You hear stories of animal abuse, and then you meet people like Gail and Rob; you say to yourself: this world is not too bad after all.

****

Glyn and Maggie live in the cottage up the hill. He is a retired water bailiff, and he and Maggie also used to run a market garden. Unfortunately he is troubled by ill health and spends most of his days indoor. A tall and slim man, now in his early 80s, Glyn is as solid as the land itself. Like most country people he is very knowledgeable on rural and farming matters. He doesn't talk about his working days much but is happy to give advice when you seek it. Maggie is short and a little bit on the round side. She has grey curls and a face that speaks jollity and wisdom, and experience of life itself. She is hospitable and dependable. Their life evolves round their large family of children, grandchildren and great grandchildren. Maggie and I are always happy to see each other. Every Christmas, for 10 years now, she makes me a huge Christmas cake, which we share with friends and families.

"I'll bring back the box, the cake base and the decorations, for next year," I say to Maggie every time when I pick up the cake, "let's recycle."

"Yes, I don't believe in wasting either," she laughs.

****

My Chinese brush painting class has just entered into its 16th year. For the first four years I ran it within the Council Adult Education programme. I pulled out when I was required to fill in mountains of paper work and my students were required to pass examinations. I decided to run it as a private concern; rent a room and charge my students at a reasonable commercial rate. It has worked. Students come and go but a core group remains.

Sue, an art teacher herself, has stayed in spite of poor health and at times personal difficulties. Jill comes and goes, depending on her health and related hospital treatment. I am always pleased when she returns after a period of absence.

Josée is one of the longest serving student. She kindly allowed me to paint her dog, a pedigree West Highland Terrier called Wilmot, and use the painting in my book *The Cat and the Tao*.

Fran is a returner. She and her daughter Michaela came to my class for a few years and then left. Then one day Fran walked into the class, it felt as if she had never been away. Fran is flamboyant in her painting. She paints big and bold. She has style. Karen likes to experiment with composition and techniques. Ann is the new addition and she has taken Chinese painting like duck to water. They came to my class with no knowledge or skills in Chinese art. Now they hold joint exhibitions regularly in local venues. I consider myself privileged to have these keen individuals working with me to keep Chinese art going in this part of the world.

Joan, Ruth, Gail, Rob, Maggie, Glyn and my students are a few of the people who have made a positive difference to my life in Wales. They are not replaceable. They are stars. I am always so glad to see them.

16. Being Foreign.

We live on a long steep hill. Our house is accessed by a narrow steep single track lane with passing spaces. I couldn't reverse up or down it to save my life. I got by and through sheer luck I managed not to drive into a ditch or crash my car into the steep bank. My luck lasted for a few years, until I had an encounter with a Mr C. He changed my driving forever.

There is a spot at the bottom of the lane where the trees are short. Locals know that the sun can blind you just at that point when you are coming up after a blind bend. I was coming home one bright summer day. I was prepared for that blinding spot, I had my sunglasses on and the sun visor down. As I came round the blind bend I was confronted by an old four wheel drive vehicle. It stopped. I too stopped my car. I know there are rules about who should reverse to make way for oncoming traffic on a steep slope, but common sense tells me whoever is closest to a passing space should reverse. So I waited, and he waited. I have heard about this man. I'll call him Mr C, not his real name. He is a local full-time farmer and a part-time widow-snatcher. He is well known and not much liked in the neighbourhood farming community for his bloody mindedness and his foul language.

After a few minutes of staring at each other through our sunglasses I decided to reverse downhill for him. It was not the easiest job as the midday sun was making the manoeuvre very difficult for someone as inexperienced as I was in reversing. As there was no passing space near me I decided to reverse up the bank, into the widest part of the lane. It seemed to me to be the right thing to do at the time, but a stupid thing to do in retrospect. I put the gear lever into reverse and started to back down. I struggled to pull to one side. I got stuck in the mud and my car stalled. The whole scenario proved to be too much for him. He got out of his car, took his sunglasses off, and started to walk towards me. I realised what I was up against. He is tall as he is broad, if he sits on me I will die an instant death. I immediately locked my car and reached for my mobile. I always know where my mobile is. I have in it the telephone numbers of the local police station, plus that of a friend who is an active member of Neighbourhood Watch. On this occasion I couldn't find it in my handbag. Then I remembered where exactly it was; it was sitting on the hallstand charging its battery.

Now we were separated by the car's side window. He bent down and we faced each other eyeball to eyeball.

I am over 5 feet tall, about 8 stones in weight, middle aged, don't work out, not trained in martial arts, have never been in the army, and do not own a weapon. The few Kung Fu moves I know I have learnt from Kung Fu Panda and Kung Fu Soccer, both box office hits. I have tried practising these moves on the males that share my home. Healey surrendered immediately and unconditionally. He rolled over, put both front paws up, and invited me to stroke his tummy. Joseph yawned and Chris just laughed. There was no way I could fight this man, blow for blow, scratch for scratch.

"You should not be allowed on the road if you can't reverse," he shouted at me over my windscreen.

There was a challenge in his voice, an instant put down. I took my sunglasses off to look at him properly. He looked unkempt, like a long haired dog that hasn't had his hair brushed by its owner for weeks. He was breathing fire, his face flushed with disgust, and the veins in his neck were pulsating with anger. I realised I was dealing with raw and negative emotions here; discrimination and rage.

Nowadays discrimination of any kind is big business. Lots of people make a living out of it; journalists, lawyers and human rights activists. Sometimes the victims themselves benefit from it too. They get compensation. Some get publicity and money from newspaper and television appearances. It is often the case that the more sensational the alleged discrimination is the bigger the money. People who are prejudiced are proud of what they do not know and are contemptuous of anyone who is different from them. Was Mr C racially abusive towards me? If he was trying to be, he had failed miserably. My view is that words, no matter how hurtful or discriminating, remain words if they fail to produce the expected response.

"Bloody foreigner," he shouted, "why don't you go home!"

"I am trying to, I live up there, but you are in the way, Mr C," I said calmly to this fireball. I believe in being polite to all mankind, at all times, especially in difficult time.

If he was surprised that I knew his name, he didn't show it. He stormed back to his car, got into the driver seat and reversed it uphill into the passing space two feet behind where he had stopped.

Have I come across racial discrimination in my life? I probably have. Do I care? No, I don't. People who discriminate make two statements about themselves; they have limited humanity and they have very limited intelligence. This sort of person's opinion of me does not mean a lot.

When you move from a big cosmopolitan city to a small hamlet in rural Wales with its small community, your ethnic origin, your mixed race marriage, your work are all unusual, do I feel fully at home? My home is where Chris is. People may define me by my skin colour, my marriage, my work, but they are saying something about themselves, not me. It is the person's character, their beliefs and values, and their civic conscience that define people. I never strive to be a local, I have lived in London most part of my adult life but I am not English. In London, I am a Chinese in London, here I am a Chinese in Wales.

Not all discriminatory behaviour is loud and in your face. A lot of it is often disguised as humour and fun. The intention is the same; to humiliate and to undermine your self belief.

I was at a function when a distinguished looking older man introduced himself to me. He told me he was a professor of Medicine and that he had spent 3 years teaching in the Medical Faculty of Hong Kong University. I was immediately interested in him. I am always delighted to meet people who have been to my hometown.

"The Chinese have an interesting way with English," he said after a few minutes of exchanging pleasantries with me. A few other guests had joined us, all apparently, keen to make his acquaintance.

"How do you mean?" I asked.

"Well, they don't seem to be able to tell the differences with some of our letters."

"Give me an example."

"They can't tell the difference between R and L, your people pronounce Robert as Lobert; and shrimps become shimps. Can you tell the difference between them?"

"Try me," I said. Our fellow guests were smiling at me.

"Can you say election?"

"Election," I said.

"Now can you replace the L with the R?" He was smirking at me.

"Do you bet I can, or I can't?" I smiled back.

"I bet you can, now prove it; say that one word to me."

Our fellow guests were no longer smiling.

"How much do you want to bet that I can?" I smiled, again.

"I bet you a fiver." Everybody watched as he took his wallet out of his inner jacket pocket. Slowly and deliberately he pulled out a five pound note. He held it in his hand.

"Bet £10. I'll give you value for money, I'll say more than one word." Our fellow guests were cheering him on. He opened his wallet again and pulled out another fiver. He handed me both notes, and he waited. I put the money in my bag.

"You want me to pronounce the R correctly in the word that you have chosen." I just wanted to be sure.

"Correct," he smiled.

"e – R-e-c-t-i-o-n." I spelled the word with emphasis on the R sound.

"I want to hear you say the word," he said.

"You wanted to hear the R sound and you've heard it. You dirty old man," I said.

I walked away without a backward glance.

Sometimes it is fun, when I see the shop assistants round here look at each other and mutter "your turn" when I walk in, then brighten up when they realise I can speak English (better than them, Chris says). Another time, almost in reverse, we were on holiday in Ireland looking at a ruin, when this oriental man came up to me and started chatting – what language, who knows, I didn't! He looked Japanese to me, why didn't I look Chinese to him? Takes all sorts!

Then there was the time in London, when my Indian neighbour complained to me that the local ironmongers were so racist.

"Racist," I said, "they're not racist, they're just rude. Reading their paper when you go in, look up after a suitable interval, and say 'Yes?' in a condescending manner?"

"Yes, that's it," Nasim said, "just rude, you think?"

"That's what Chris says, they're just as rude to him. I don't let them get away with it. I ask them if they're serving as soon as I go in, and get them running for what I want. Don't give them an inch." Nasim giggled nervously, trying to imagine herself doing the same, and failing.

Here, I was the only foreigner in this small hillside community (an Egyptian colleague of Chris's has moved nearby now). I am probably the only adult Chinese who does not work in Chinese takeaways, restaurants or laundrettes in this town. A research report conducted by a social psychologist concludes that people are suspicious of foreigners partly because of their accents. A strong or thick accent is less trusted because it is a barrier to communication and understanding. Well, I speak with an accent, not thick, not subtle, but a unique southern Chinese accent. No one has yet told me that they find me untrustworthy or difficult to understand. Actually a foreign accent can work to your advantage.

Shortly after we moved to Wales we went to a local ironmongers/DIY shop to buy a Hoover. They didn't have in stock the model we wanted. They ordered it for us and the manager, Paul, said he would telephone when it arrived. Two weeks passed and he didn't ring. So I decided to call him. "Can I speak to the manager please?" I said. A voice with a strong Welsh accent sang down the phone, "Hello, Mrs H, I was about to call you, your Hoover has just arrived. Oh dear, you sound awful, have you got a cold?"

I had not told him who I was, and had a very bad cold at the time: my Chinese accent still came through loud and clear to a local Welshman.

You see, your uniqueness can make you memorable.

When I speak to people on the telephone for the first time I often take step to engage them. When he tells me his name is Paul, I would say, "May I call you Paul?" When he says his name is Paul Jones, I address him as Mr Jones. Some may think this is old-fashioned courtesy, but I am an old-fashioned sort of person. This way I find I always get positive response. I never attempt to change my accent.

Have a foreign face though, can be a very different matter. It can be very confusing to some people as I have found out on one autumn day. I had finished work and was about to make a cup of tea when there was a knock on the front door. I went to answer and was confronted by too very middle-age women, both dressed in light woollen cardigans, tweed below knee skirts and solid leather shoes. They both held books in their hands. They looked at me for a few seconds and then smiled.

"Can we talk to you about our God?" one asked.

"You can't. I am a Buddhist," I replied.

"Oh, very well, thank you and good bye." They left.

I returned to make my tea. Someone was knocking at the porch door. I went to answer and there were the two women again. They looked at me for a few seconds and smiled.

"Can we talk to you about our God?" one asked.

"No, you can't. I am a Taoist," I said.

"Oh, sorry to bother you. Good bye." They left. Had they realised I was the same person they spoke to one minute ago?

I went back to make my tea. Someone knocked at the door, the back door this time. I went to answer it. It was the two ladies again. They had climbed over the gate and had come to the garden side.

They looked at me for a few seconds and smiled.

"Can we talk to you about our God?" one asked.

"No, you can't. I am a follower of Confucius," I said. I was mystified. Had my face changed in the last few minutes. They didn't seem to recognise me from a moment ago, three times.

"The trouble with you Chinese is that you all look the same," Chris said over dinner.

"What, all the 1.4 billion of us!"

"Yes," Chris laughed.

****

Mr C was a trigger. The final push came when Ruth had her house renovated. Tons of building materials were delivered in multi-ton lorries up the narrow mountain lane. The lorry drivers came with diplomatic immunity; they didn't do reversing and wouldn't do it. They knew no other drivers dared argue with the size of their lorry.

"You have to reverse, love, I can't do it," one lorry driver shouted.

"You have to go back, love, I won't do it," another shouted.

I made up my mind to learn to reverse. I practised it on our own sloping drive. Up I drove and down I reversed. I then reversed up and drove back down. I practised in both my car and Chris's. I knew no technique, it was blind reversing with the car windows down, driver door half opened and my hair flying. In the process I left some dramatic patterns on the immaculate lawn and sent the cats running. I nearly crashed into the trees that lined our drive. I sent Chris's patience flying. "No driving on the grass," he shouted, "come, let me show you how it is done." He got into the passenger seat, "look, have the window down if you must but for goodness sake shut the car door." He taught me how to reverse using the wing mirrors. I had always wondered what those little mirrors were for.

"And those mirrors are not for putting lipstick on," Chris shouted.

Now when I see a car coming towards me in the lane, whether uphill or down, I usually make the first move to reverse, and it is so much easier.

People like Mr C and the lorry drivers have disappeared from my life forever. Meteors don't stay long.

17. Two Brothers, One Man.

The kittens grew up to be beautiful and strong cats. Every day their confidence grew. They learned to master the outdoors, and they learned to trust us.

Joseph was tall and athletic with a most boisterous and fearless personality. He would challenge anything that moved, and climb anything that stood still. Rocco was sleek, tall, dark and handsome. While Joseph hunted rabbits and hedgehogs, he danced with butterflies and bees. He was dressed from head to toe in black, complete with black whiskers and a tiny white bow tie under his chin. He was the ultimate feline Fred Astaire, elegant, handsome and charming. Rocco dazzled everyone who set eyes upon him. He dazzled me.

Rocco spent most of his time contemplating philosophy. There was nothing he liked better than to sit in front of the fire, whisky in one hand and a cigar in the other, discussing life issues with whoever happened to be around. I loved Rocco. He was the most affectionate of my three cats, the only cat that allowed me to stroke his armpits!

When I touched him he would immediately stand up, purr thunderously, telling me he was delighted that I noticed him. There was a game we both enjoyed and played often; you see, for reasons I didn't understand, Rocco, when lying flat, looked longer than my other two cats. When he stretched right out he measured well over three feet from the tip of his ears to the tail. I could rotate him like a rope, or arrange him like a serpent. And you know what? He let me! Joseph would bite my hands off, and H would simply say, *"Don't be so daft, behave yourself, woman!"*

Rocco was also the most vulnerable of my three cats. He was born to be a philosopher and a gentleman. Aggression he knew nothing about. I recalled an encounter he had with Eli, a stray tom from hell.

I was weeding in the rockery when suddenly I heard a deep growl. Looking round I saw a scarecrow look-alike of a cat at about six yards away. He was circling Rocco, then about 4 months old. This cat, whom I named Eli, was staring menacingly and growling threateningly at my baby! Rocco did not have the knowledge or experience to deal with this kind of aggression, he was reduced to a lump of jelly, rooted to the spot. I rushed to the crime scene waving my arms like a mad woman and shouting, "You baby snatcher, leave him alone or I'll slit your throat and bite your nose off." He obviously didn't fancy having his nose bitten off, so he spat at Rocco before disappearing behind some thick bushes. Chris witnessed this heroic rescue from the other side of the garden. He informed me later that I had done what a mother cat would have done to protect the kitten. He was very proud of me. We had not seen the last of Eli, for he would return later to cause more chaos in the hamlet.

****

Healey allowed Rocco into his personal space. They would often sit together like two book ends, dozing, sunbathing or just watching Joseph going about his battles with leaves and birds. The three cats ate together. In winter they slept together in the porch. In summer they preferred the cooler roof space of the garage. We extended the sleeping area there with more boxes and straw.

Sadly, though, Rocco left home when he was two years old. We supposed he didn't like the terms and conditions. I could discuss philosophy with him but I couldn't provide him with what he wanted: to be a full time indoor cat. The cats stayed indoors part time only. The arrangement suited Healey and

Joseph but not Rocco. Lately the two brothers had started to fight a lot, with Joseph usually starting it, and winning most of the time. As a Chinese proverb goes: *Two tigers cannot share one mountain and two dragons cannot share the same water.* When chucking out time came Rocco would hide. He made it clear that he didn't want to go outside. Rocco was not happy. He started to disappear during feeding time. I suspected that someone up the hill was poaching him. They probably enticed him with whisky, cigar and the fireplace! After a few months of "on and off" with us, one day he disappeared completely, just did not come back. It broke my heart. After all the affection and care I gave him, he just picked himself up and left.

My heart ached with the longing to see that sleek little cat again. The few weeks after Rocco's departure I was in denial. I refused to believe that he'd gone. He would come back, I told myself. I extended my morning and evening walk in the field in the hope that I would be there to greet him when he returned. When he failed to appear I thought he had been run over by a car, he was dead, his body rotting in a ditch.

We decided not to go on television to appeal for his return, nor to search every inch of the hillside. Where would we begin when we were surrounded by acres of farmland, all privately owned? The most upsetting aspect was the "not knowing" what had happened, although the pattern of his disappearance strongly suggested that someone had poached him from us.

Then I got very angry: he was an ungrateful soul, my love and affection had meant nothing to him. H said I should forget about him, as he had already forgotten me: he was right. Rocco was not worth it! Then I thought; how could I blame him, he was not happy here, why shouldn't he go in search of greener pasture. Cats know about moving on.

I know the cause and effects of human separation. I didn't expect the departure of little Rocco would cause me such grief. It was more than a year before I finally accepted that he was gone forever. I must admit there are still moments when I look out to the horizon and dream about Rocco coming home. We'd had such happy times together.

I had no doubt Rocco had loved me. But his love was conditional; he wanted to be a full time indoor cat. My fear of cats, although largely cured, would not allow me to meet his demand. I had failed him. I know and understand the equation of human love: to give a lot and take your fair share. I didn't know this applies to cats too. I'd learnt my lesson. I will always remember Rocco, a handsome cat with black whiskers and beautiful eyes that smile like a little boy. A cat that dazzled me.

When affinity ends, fate changes course.

(Anon)

****

"I wish I had treated Rocco differently. It is all my fault that he left home."

"*May be he has gone to visit Mama,*" Joseph meowed.

"Don't blame yourself, love, when a cat wants to leave home there is nothing you can do to hold him back. Isn't that right, Healey?" Chris glanced at H.

"*He has already forgotten you, he is a cat,*" Healey said to me, and blinked.

"*Can I have his f—o—o—d as well?*" Joseph purred wildly by my feet. He certainly had no difficulty forgetting.

Healey's return, and now Rocco's departure, have taught me something about cats: of all domestic pets, I think cats are the only one that have the intelligence to make choices, and the ability and toughness to act on them. I've learnt a lesson.

Don't take cats for granted. We have modified part of the house to give Healey and Joseph full indoor access to that part soon after Rocco's departure, too late, alas. I knew the real barrier lay within me. I still had a rush of adrenaline when the cats stayed too close for too long; I still feared them. I vowed to strive to rid myself of the last trace of cat phobia in my blood. Rocco had taught me a big lesson.

No one is faultless:
Those who have the courage to admit their mistakes,
And are willing to learn from them,
Are indeed wise.

(Feng Menglong)

****

Joseph had grown into a gladiator cat. Tall, fearless and imposing, he was athletic and had great physical presence. He had also retained some of his kitten-like characteristics: boisterous, mischievous and a devil-may-care attitude. If he was a human, he would be the cowboy hero, with fast gun and a face that showed he never forgot a favour, or a grievance. You wouldn't cross him. H was approaching the wrong side of 60 (cat years), and was spending more time in meditation. With Rocco gone, H had become more tolerant of Joseph. They slept together in a big basket, and ate side by side, with Joseph sitting down and Healey standing up.

Joseph is Chris's cat. They are great mates and they share a few things. They both like digging and singing outdoors. On a sunny day Chris would be digging his vegetable patch and singing his heart out. A few yards away Joseph would be clawing hard at a mole hill and shouting his lungs out, *"You make me work so hard to catch you. When I do I'll eat you, let me tell you, it will be very messy for both of us!"*

105

They both like their food. At feeding time Joseph would finish his own food first. He would then shoulder Healey out of the way and would eat his. I am a slow eater and Chris always finishes his food before me. Thank heavens that he hasn't (yet) gone as far as to elbow me away from the dining table and finish my food, though he sometimes finishes mine off if I leave a bit. Chris's love of good food shows in his effort to find good ingredients and interesting recipes. Joseph is undiscriminating; he eats virtually everything that he has caught: rabbits, voles, mice and even squirrels (he draws the line at eating claws, and gall bladders, and once left the only rat we have seen here lying dead, uneaten). I cut corners and would happily substitute tomatoes for basil in my cooking. What is the difference? They are both vegetables, and they go down the same way.

They love to power nap. Joseph is a natural, he would nap anywhere that is warm and cosy. Chris has acquired the habit and skill to power nap in his junior doctor days when 24/7 work pattern required him to grab whatever sleep he could, anywhere, at any time in (almost) any position. Now cat and man often power nap together; Joseph in Chris's lap and Chris in the recliner-chair's lap (Chris asks me why I call it a power nap: however much he does it, he never seems to get any power).

I still can't let the cats sit on my lap, but my suspicion and fear of cats has grown steadily less over the years. I have become almost totally at ease with them. With my new found confidence and understanding of cats, I decided to write and paint my second cat book: *The Philosopher Cat.*

"Why do I look so small in it?" I was sketching in the garden when Joseph came over to see what I was doing. He spotted himself in a corner of my sketch.

"My darling, you may be small but you are a very important part of the picture," I stroked him and he purred wildly.

Painting is not a job or a career to me, it is a way of life. The process itself is like building a community. A painting is the sum of many small parts. Each part has its unique value to the total scene. Likewise we are all a small part of a big picture. We may not be able to see our significance from where we stand, but without individuals there is no community and without community there is no society.

My second book was published two years after the first. On the day it was released my publisher sent me a big bunch of flowers. I showed Chris an advance copy of the book. The cats saw it too. Joseph went wild, *"Look, there is me. Oh, there is me AGAIN!"*

That evening Joseph was late for his supper, something that was never allowed to happen by his own rule.

"He is going round telling everybody about HIS book. He told them he has written and painted the book himself," H explained.

"Oh dear, fame has gone into his head," I said.

Half an hour later he dashed in through the cat flap yelling *"f—o—o—d."*

He looked very pleased with himself.

Chris and Joseph are firm friends. They know each other's hearts and they read each other's minds. When cat looks at man in a certain way, man's lap immediately stretches out to accommodate cat. When man wants to get up to fetch something, cat would jump down and wait by the recliner. They have perfected the skill of mind reading.

There is a saying by Bai Juyi, a great poet of ancient time, on friendship:

To choose a friend is no easy matter,
For both of you have to be skilled in mind reading.

18. The Art of War.

Birds with the same wings fly together,
Animals with the same paws hunt together.

(Chinese proverb)

That proverb is not true of cats. Cats fear and reject each other. They will fight tooth and nail for females and fight to defend their own territories. Cat books tell me that when two stranger cats meet, most normal cats would defuse their aggression by subtle adjustments of their body language. 98% of cats would break away without exchanging a blow. Healey and Joseph belonged to the last 2%.

When confronted with an intruding cat, Joseph would immediately plug himself into that invisible battery. He would fluff out to an astonishing size with a fighting ridge on his back. With eyes wide opened and tail brushed he would spring at his enemy, scramble onto his head and go about biting and scratching without mercy.

"Get out of my garden, you scum of the earth!" he would bawl.

The cat fight of the year would rage with growls and spits and fur flying. In true commando spirit Joseph would never decline a challenge. He would fight decisively to secure a quick victory. He is the kind of cat you want around if your home is threatened by a passing stray.

Joseph was young and strong, he had sufficient power and drive to win, and he would challenge until the intruder could not help but engage. Joseph usually came out victorious. Occasionally, he came home with cuts and scratches, but a visit to the vet and a course of antibiotics later, he was ready to face any alien cats again.

Sun Tse, a military genius who wrote *The Art of War* over 2,300 years ago has a saying about Joseph:

Good at attack, your enemy does not know how to defend:
In any battle, victory matters, not lengthy confrontation.

Joseph fought like a gladiator, he would fight fiercely to win fast. *"He is lucky, he is born with energy for at least 10 cats,"* H said.

****

The dynamic changed when Polar Bear came on the scene. His real name was Boris and he belonged to Claire, our other neighbour. In his first life Boris had lived with a family down in the valley. He was unruly and was vicious towards the children and the mother had to get rid of him. Claire took him on.

My cats and I called him Polar Bear because he looked like one. He was dressed in white, from the tip of his ears to the tip of his tail. He had a big fat face that made his eyes look tiny. He also had a black splodge on his nose that made him look a bit dim, and as if he hadn't cleaned himself for days. Polar Bear liked to play rough. Posing as a street fighter, he would sit on fences and window ledges hours on end to invite fights. Joseph never disappointed. He always rose to the invitation.

"Who are you looking at?" Polar Bear would inquire menacingly.

"You, sunshine. I don't like the dirt on your nose, filth!" Joseph stuck his tongue out.

I saw big trouble coming, "Joseph, come home immediately," I yelled at him.

"Are you crazy, he is my mortal enemy." Joseph was very confident about his fighting talent, he once boasted to H, *"I*

am so strong I can easily give half of it away and still have enough strength left for myself to win every battle." That was before he met Polar Bear, who was a lot younger.

Cats don't fight because it is good against evil, nor is it about balance of power. They are created by the same Great Hand; they share the same DNA, the same adrenaline, and the same inbuilt dislike of one another. They fight because they just can't stand one another. My conclusion is that when cats fight it is simply a case of one set of DNA against another set of DNA.

The battle began. Black and white bodies blurred into one. With fur flying, the two mortal enemies matched each other paw to paw, tooth to tooth and claw to claw. I tried separating them with a broom. I threw water over them. They just moved on to another field, there they continued their battle. H came to stand beside me.

"I wish they would stop."

"They've started, so they'll finish," H said sagely.

"H, go to help Joseph out," I pleaded with the sage.

"Dogs and humans do gang warfare. Cats don't, we fight one to one, fair and square."

At sunset Joseph came home. He slept for three days; getting up to drink a little, eat a little and go outside to the toilet a little. Two days later we discovered a huge abscess below the corner of his right eye which required drainage. Off we took him to the vet. A course of antibiotics later he was ready to fight Polar Bear again. According to Healey, Polar Bear also slept for three days; getting up to drink a little, eat a little and use the litter tray a little. He had multiple bite wounds on the back of his neck which also required a trip to the vet and a course of antibiotics.

"How do you know this?" I asked H.

"I can't tell you, it is secret of the trade. We cats are good spies," he said sagely.

At the time of writing Joseph and Polar Bear still meet occasionally to compare Kung Fu techniques. They still hurt each other. Neither knows how to sustain lasting victory. Their owners still have to pay an arm and a leg to repair the damage.

****

Sun Tse has a saying about Healey too:

The best victory is one that is won without fighting.

Healey's war strategy demonstrated this to good effect. When he saw a stray cat in HIS territory, he would go after it. He never went faster than walking, but would follow it confidently, swiftly and as far as necessary until the intruder disappeared. He would then roll back calmly with not a whisker out of place. H was not a timid cat, he would investigate any strange noise and any mysterious shadows in his territory.

One day while working in the studio I looked out of the window and saw H in the garden. Two feet away from him an ugly and huge cat from outer space was inviting him to a duel. With his back arched, the alien was walking sideway like a blown up crab, spitting and threatening to scratch H's eye out. I rushed out, armed with my biggest painting brush. I was determined to brush this cat off the face of the earth. I stopped at the door. Something told me my cat was all right.

H didn't shake with fright or lie on his back to admit inferiority as you might expect. He just sat there like an immovable rock, with all four paws and tail tucked neatly underneath. As cool as a cucumber, he proceeded to read the lawn with half closed eyes. The alien cat danced closer, *"Come on, you coward, get up and fight like a cat, play extinction later!"* he hissed. H didn't move. Direct challenge didn't work, and the alien decided to use the 3D insults to humiliate H.

"Are you deaf? Are you dumb? Are you dead!" the alien growled. Human beings would see that as the biggest insult of all time. But H carried on reading the lawn. At this point the alien looked truly puzzled. *"I am not going to fight you, you are not worth it!"* He spat at Healey and then turned his back, looking over his shoulders a few times at the rock before disappearing back into outer space.

H never wanted to be top cat. I had never seen him in a fight with anyone; cat or dog. By staying calm, and showing it, he had successfully deterred the enemy. He drove the opponent away without having to lift one paw.

This strategy is well documented in Chinese classics. Here is one example:

When you are in danger, lie low, mind your words and be cautious;
This is self preservation.
You will not win a glorious victory, but you will avoid a great disaster.

(I-Ching, The Book of Changes)

"H, you are a crafty old cat! You didn't move an inch and you have won." I couldn't hide my pride in Healey's peaceful victory. It was impossible not to be impressed by this cool performance. But he rejected my conclusion.

"He is twice my size and probably half my age. Fight him? You must be joking. I am not stupid," H meowed.

****

Villains come out of the dark the world over,
They are not on anybody's side but their own.

(Chinese proverb)

Heroes have their wisdom and strategies, but thugs have their own cunning and deadly plots too. Occasionally the odd stray wanders onto our land, with unfriendly intentions on his mind. I often give them a name, and sketch their mug shots for the identity parade. And here is the story of Eli, without whom the feline "art of war" wouldn't be complete. I remember Eli well. He was the stray tom that reduced Rocco to a lump of jelly when he was a kitten.

Like a villain in a spaghetti western, Eli returned to the hamlet one day with guns in his paws and a stick of dynamite between his teeth. This time he wasn't just passing through. He had a mission: to beat up every single tom and to conquer every queen in this neighbourhood. There was a stench in the air and all the cats smelled danger. The vet bills went up. He was so elusive that no one had seen him, except me, at a distance. He was a short hair mixed brown/yellow/white cat. Thin like a scarecrow, with a square head and chest, but gnawed limbs.

He had made himself at home in my garden. He was so arrogant, he didn't bother to make himself inconspicuous, but walked right down the middle of the garden path as though he was the flag bearer in a victory parade. If my cats would not take him on, I would.

I had considered contacting the RSPCA. They could set a trap to catch him. They could separate him from his testicles to make a real man of him, and they could find a home for him. But who would want to take on a feral psycho? Would I want to confine this free spirit to a cage where he would probably die of old age? I have seen big cats in zoos. My heart cries when I see these big, proud beasts pacing their cages, waiting to be fed, and doing their job of entertaining visitors. In my cat phobic days I would have had no hesitation in getting the RSPCA involved. These days I love cats and admire many of their attributes. I couldn't bring myself to trap and imprison any cat.

Whenever I saw Eli, I shouted and threw stones at him (I always miss!) He ignored me. Then one day we had a close encounter. I was reading in the garden. Joseph and Healey were sleeping elsewhere. I looked round and there was Eli coming down the drive. I got up slowly and moved towards the garden hose. Silently I turned it on and set the spray gun at jet mode. I turned to drown him, but he was gone. Spray gun in hand, I looked for him under trees and bushes. Suddenly I heard a hissing noise, like a leak from a gas pipe. I turned and came face to face with the ugliest, meanest cat I've ever seen. He was there, back arched, tail raised, matted fur standing on end as if he was receiving an electric shock. His mean lips were pulled back to reveal a mouthful of uneven, shark like teeth, his thin face was contorted into an evil grimace. He was a poster boy for feral cats. It was like seeing the scariest villain in a movie. That was when I thought of Eli Wallach in the spaghetti westerns. You knew he was horrible and ugly, but you had to look at him. That was exactly what I did.

He had left the path and come round the back way to catch me unawares! We were six feet apart. I forgot the spray gun in my hand. His ugliness and cunning had stunned me. He looked like a hyena about to attack, his back arched, his fur dirty and matted with mud, he growled. His eyes were full of hatred and he hissed, *"Come on human, where are the handcuffs?"*

I felt a chill down my spine. This cat was vicious. What had happened to him? Thoughts flashed through my mind. He must have been handsome once. Was he ever loved? Did he ever sleep in front of a fire on winter evenings? Had he tasted roast chicken and warm milk? The hardship of living rough, on the edge, had left scars all over him. One of his eyes was oozing pus, his ears were scarred, his nose deformed. Each scar told a story, of victory or defeat. And he had been hungry and cold, with fleas and illness. Suddenly I felt very sorry for him. Moving slowly and still keeping an eye on him, I wound up the garden hose. "Go away, I'll let you off this time," I said.

I thought about Eli and other feral cats. The lucky ones live in a feral colony, others carry on the family tradition of roaming the land. They survive on their wits. They have no attachments and trust no one. Eventually they die a lonely and often painful death as do all wild animals. I asked Healey why Eli lived the life he did.

"Freedom. He is as free as the wind," H purred softly.

"But what a life!"

"He is free to hunt, to come and go as he wishes, to do whatever he likes. He is the wind," H explained in the carefully considered manner of a sage.

"H, do you want to be as free as the wind?" I asked softly.

"No, the wind does not know everything. I don't know everything either, but I know my destiny and I've found it. I am very contented," H said sagely.

The wind blows across this land freely. It comes from nowhere and goes nowhere. It has no birth place and no death bed. It knows no friends, no love, no passion and no sorrow. Yes, the wind may be free, but it doesn't know everything.

****

Eli continued to terrorise the hamlet with fear and fight. Cats were coming home wounded. Chris decided to do something. His chance came. One Sunday morning we saw Eli walking down the steep path in our field, tough and bold as you like. Chris got out his shotgun and went over. I said, *"Don't kill him."* Chris replied, *"Hm."*

I followed, but stopped at the fence gate. Our two cats were nowhere to be seen. To my astonishment, Chris didn't sneak up to Eli, he stepped out into his field of vision and called out before he fired. Eli fled, as fast as a cat could go, and Chris fired a shot over his head.

Two things happened simultaneously, when the gun went off. Healey dashed out of the undergrowth and headed straight for the garage, in through the cat flap without touching the sides, and wasn't seen until dinner time. Joseph jumped six feet in the air from concealment in long grass, six feet straight up, and then dived into undergrowth, yelling, *"Total madness, he nearly killed me!"*

"You warned him, didn't you?" I said to Chris.

"Yes, I had to give him a warning. He needed to know what was happening." He took a sip of chilled wine. "And besides, I didn't shoot at him, I shot over his head, just to frighten him off. It would take a lot to make me shoot a cat."

Still, we saw no more of Eli. I had to admit he was a memorable villain. Chris didn't kill or punish him, he didn't have to; villains will subdue one another.

When you harm others you also harm yourself,
For evils always find their way back to the doer.

(Chinese proverb)

19. A Few Things about Cats

When you love someone, beware of his weaknesses;
When you dislike someone, beware of his strengths.

(Confucius)

Devoted cat lovers would understand Confucius's sentiment on love, because it applies to cats too. Some cats are wise, others silly; some are courageous, others timid; some are affectionate, others aloof. The list will go on, but they all share a few common characteristics which make them unique in the animal world. Non-obedience is one of them. This gene is not erasable by training or any form of psychotherapy.

I often TRIED to call the cats in at night. More often than not Healey would look at me soulfully as if to say, *"I wish I could obey you but I can't, I am a cat,"* and he would shrug and set off into the darkness, I knew not where. Joseph would simply say, "Nobody tells me what to do; if they do I'll do the opposite." They don't do anything I ask but expect me to do EVERYTHING they ask: *f—o—o—d, more f—o—o—d, open the door to let me in, open the door to let me out, open the door to let me in again.* Cats hand out orders and humans make requests. If my requests sound too "order-like", Rocco would rush outside to consult the beans and peas about it; Joseph would sweep it under the carpet; H would simply pass my order down the line to his tail. Over the years I have managed to train them to respond to the ringing of a bowl as a signal that food is being served and would your lordships please return. Its effectiveness depends on where they are and how many rabbits they have eaten. On the whole it works. Healey and Rocco would come in purring, not Joseph.

"All this shouting and yelling, yelling and screaming, and the bowl RINGING! It really is quite unnecessary. The neighbours

are talking," he meowed before diving into a big plate of food.

Once out of the cat flap, they are their own. You have no access to them and have no way of knowing where they have gone. They wander out at will and leave you to worry about them. Hours later they would wander in casually demanding food and your attention. They demand freedom and will not give a moment's thought to your concern and feelings. They are selfish, single minded and believe in their right to do anything and go anywhere they want. There is a passage in *The Roots of Wisdom*:

> *When hungry they cling to you for food,*
> *When full they shun you.*
> *Where there is warmth, they throw themselves at you,*
> *Where there is cold they spurn you.*
> *These are common flaws in human nature.*
>
> (Hung Ying-ming).

These are ALSO the common flaws in cat nature!

****

The "man who understands cats" occasionally gets bitten by Joseph. He doesn't seem to mind. "Cats are cats, they never plan to bite, they just react," he speaks in the cat's defence. Chris would be gently stroking Joseph. He (the cat!) would purr wildly, then in a flash he would growl and grab Chris's hand with all four sets of claws out, and sink his teeth into the man's flesh. He would then just leave the room slowly with no obvious concern, no regret and no guilt. He just walks away – totally indifferent.

Chris gets bitten because he gets too close and because he feels confident with cats. I don't have to experience it to know cats have a tight grip and sharp claws, powerful and can injure you. I have also learnt that cats are unpredictable. Joseph is big and strong and he has a fiery temper. I am cautious, when I feel he has had enough of being stroked, I am quick to stop and get out of the way. I get the occasional superficial scratches. I stroke him, but I never get so close or affectionate enough for him to react; to bite me.

Some people behave like cats. They flatter and entice you, lead you on until suddenly they realise you are too close. You have entered their personal safety zone and they feel threatened. They flee, only to compose themselves a little further on and look at you enticingly, inviting you to come closer again. Like cats, these people treat relationships totally and utterly on their own terms.

****

I have also observed interesting aspects of cat's behaviour which link them to my Chinese mind. Like reclusive sages in ancient times, cats aspire to a contemplative life. They are so laid back yet so inscrutable that I attribute wisdom and human thoughts to them. Of all domestic animals, cats alone have an aura of inscrutability. When a cat looks at you, he is saying to you, *"I know everything about you and you know nothing about me."* I am convinced that my cats have opinions of me, but they don't tell: I probably wouldn't want to hear it either! This *"I know but I won't tell, not even if you give me all the tea in China "* attitude seems to demonstrate the highest level of integrity and virtue, characteristics greatly revered by cultured and honourable men of ancient China. Anyone who claims they have never seen a cat looking inscrutable is either unobservant to a fault or has nothing that the cats find worth noting.

Cats are nobody's fool! They coolly survey the world. They speak to the world eloquently with one word, *meow,* and the world listens and responds. This single word is so powerful that even if cats were born to speak a thousand words, I am convinced they wouldn't speak them. Why bother? After all, "A good talker uses very few words," said Mencius (371-289 BC), one of China's great philosophers.

Cats are curious and inquisitive. They will leave no box unturned, no hole un-poked, no smell or noise un-investigated. They walk about with their tails held in a question mark, telling the world that they want answers: who is hiding in that hole? What is in that empty box? Like disciples of ancient masters, they too want truth and enlightenment. Curiosity may kill a cat, but information will surely bring it back.

Cats have guts and they have backbone. I watch as my cats bend, arch, rotate and twist their malleable bodies into any shape they like at will: a ball, a U, an S, a figure of eight and many more. And you know what? They never complain of back pain or suffer from a broken spine. Cats are like an upright bamboo that bends in the wind but never gets broken. This ability to "bend and stretch" demonstrates a flexibility to adapt to life's atrocities while keeping one's backbone intact; an essential virtue of an upright person. Cats are blessed with this enviable ability.

I conclude that cats are intelligent and un-trainable, muted and eloquent, primitive and lordly, proud and ungrateful, indolent and vigilant, affectionate and mocking, funny and un-yielding, enticing and solitary, all at the same time.

Healey and Joseph are my cats but they do not belong to me. It would probably be more appropriate to say that they own me, much to my good fortune. I greet them gladly when they roll back from their wanderings. I offer them my home and I fill their food bowl to the brim. In return they reward me with their purring songs and allow me to stroke their silky fur.

They look at me with big green eyes that hold all their secrets which they will never tell. All I ask is that they return to me. How can I not love my cats?

20. A Cat Dies.

Life is changing all the time,
No one can forecast its course.

(Anon)

When the weather permitted, Healey and I often sat in the garden. Together we watched the antics of birds and butterflies, clouds and mist and the passing of the seasons. He connected me to the land in a way I had not appreciated previously. Somehow the land with its trees, flowers, autumn leaves and spring bulbs all looked better with a black cat about.

I was getting used to being owned by a cat. I learnt to read his body language and knew exactly when he wanted to eat, to go out, and to come back in. Working at home I had the opportunity to observe his behaviour. He was so low key that he could have been on sedatives all the time. He had an odd way of sleeping under the radiator, with all four paws sticking up in the air, and not moved for hours on end. I sometimes wondered if he had died? When I checked on him he would not move his body, but his eyes would flick open and his head revolve. His eyes would follow me around like the movement of the red detecting light in our burglar alarm sensor.

We also watched each other. I never found out what he saw in me. I suppose certain things in life are better left unexplained. The company of this magnificent person in cat fur had made a positive contribution to my life. H and I seemed to be united in some way which I did not fully understand. I only knew it was precious to both of us. My mother would have attributed this to fate. Well, fate certainly smiled on me when H returned to his land all those years ago.

During a routine health check the vet found nodules on Healey's abdomen. He took a biopsy and sent it for histology.

A week later we got the result. It was very bad news; H had a most aggressive form of cancer. It was one that would spread very quickly, probably to his lungs. He only had months to live. The prospect ahead was real. What happened when a cat was "dying"? Would he know? What would he want? I asked myself.

What are my feelings about death? To die today is probably no worse than dying tomorrow or the day after. Personally I am not afraid of dying as long as it is not pre-mature or violent. I know what I want; I want to live in my own home until the very end and to die in the company of the people I love and trust. Would H want the same? It frightened me to think that death was just around the corner and would take him away from me when the time came. Would it cause much pain and suffering to H? "What happens when a cat dies?" Would it be like switching off the television and the screen turns black? Or would it be like turning off the light and the room goes dark?

I had thought that I knew everything about Healey, but he had kept this one from me.

When people you love die, they leave a hole in your life, will it be the same when your cat dies? I had become so used to him, to his mood and expression, his meows and his greeting routine. I knew he was only a cat, he wasn't everything, but then he'd been part of the furniture, part of my daily routine, and even part of me, how do you bid farewell to part of you.

In his 12th year he had begun to move slowly. He had given up hunting. He was turning into an old man. My cat and I were getting old together. Chris did not do pondering over life and death, he did enough of it at work, so he told me. But I, like most women, ponder a lot over many things in life. Healey's incurable illness made me ponder a lot over ageing and dying. We became firm partners in pondering. I would sit on the floor with him, and I would ponder silently. He would sit still and look pensive. I could only guess that he was pondering , although I had no way of knowing what he was thinking about. He looked grave and serious as if he understood my thoughts. Then he would get up and walk away quietly when he'd had enough of pondering.

No words could describe how I felt. I had to tell the cat. It had become the most natural thing for me to talk to him. I found him under my chair in the studio. I sat on the carpet by him. I didn't know how to start, so I started with my own death.

"H, look, this is fantasy, what would you do if I were to die tomorrow?"

"I will stay here until I also die. The fox may take my body but my spirit will go to seek yours out until I find you," Healey blinked.

"I fear for you, my Darling, you are not well."

"What is your fear? I am still alive."

"I fear that you may suffer, I fear I am going to lose you."

"I am not suffering now and I am still alive. What's your problem?"

"I promise I will take care of you, I will not allow you to suffer."

"You mean you will end my life with euthanasia?"

"Yes." I was surprised at his grasp of my thinking.

"But why? Dying is a very ordinary event. It has to be because it happens all the time."

"Why? My darling, it is because I love you." I started to sob.

He rolled over, *"Come on, pull my whiskers, scratch my ears, it will make you feel better."*

I bent down to stroke him and I saw those ugly cancerous nodules in his abdomen. I felt worse. Part of my heart had already gone. I swallowed hard.

"You behave as if you have already buried me! I am still here, TODAY," Healey purred gently.

Why can't we be like a cat, to live for the present with no imaginary fear or irrational fantasy? Why can't we make today the most important day of our life, like cats do.

"If you come back in your next life as a cat again, will you come back to me?"

"No."

"Why not?" I felt a bit hurt.

"I'll wait for you on the top of the rainbow, you join me there when your time comes."

"I'll take my time."

"Don't rush to join me. We cats are very patient."

****

He was coming to the end of his life's journey. When he died would he become a thing of the past and never be brought to mind? How would I remember him? I didn't know the answers to these questions. I had never had a cat that died on me before. In fact I'd never had a cat before H. This was my first hand experience of a seriously ill and much loved cat. All I knew was that I still could touch him, stroke his whiskers and hear him purr. I would enjoy these subtle pleasures when I still could. I had to think like a cat: enjoy today, NOW is all that matters. A wise man of ancient time said:

If you accept that what is born must eventually die,
Then the path that leads to the end of life does not have to be too demanding.

The path to the last post can be a slow, painful and lonely one for the dying. I would endeavour to prolong Healey's path, and to make it as smooth and as pain free as possible for him. And when the end came I would be there to hold his paws and stroke his whiskers when he took his last breath.

Love comes in many shapes and forms. Loss is loss whether it is an animal or human. The death of a much loved pet brings great sadness but the experience is far less conflicting. The loss of a human is much more complex, it brings into play a mixture of emotions like love, grief, regrets, guilt, and for some, unresolved conflicts, remorse and unspoken apologies.

****

In the coming weeks the impending death of this special friend made me re-examine my past behaviour towards the deaths of my parents and find it wanting. My father died years before my mother. I wasn't there for either of them when they were dying, to hold their hands or to offer comfort. I was nine thousand miles away when they took their last breath. I flew back for my mother's funeral. I didn't for my father.

It was six months later during daffodil time when the cancer took final hold. It had got to Healey's lungs. Chris and Joseph were watching television together. H was sleeping under the sofa. I was reading in my armchair when H got up and walked slowly towards me.

"Can I sit on your lap?" He sat upright by my feet and meowed.

"No, H, you know you can't." All my cats know that I don't do lap top cats. Joseph and Rocco had tried to jump on my lap. My reaction was so violent that they jumped off immediately and had never attempted to do it again. H, on the other hand, had never tried. He knew I couldn't handle a cat at such close quarters. Why was he asking now? With hindsight I know now that he asked because he knew it was to be our final evening together.

I got up and moved to the radiator, sat down and signalled him to join me. He came and lay down beside me. I rested my hand on him and we both dozed off. I woke up suddenly; I heard something that sounded like a small engine running. Healey woke up too. He was standing there, his breathing shallow and noisy. That engine noise came from his chest. It was sudden and quick. One minute he was warming himself under the radiator, the next he had to breathe sitting up. His laboured breathing sounded like a steam engine. Was he suffering? Was he frightened? I once had a very bad chest infection while visiting my family in Hong Kong. I panicked as I struggled to breathe. It was a very frightening experience. I didn't want H to suffer, I didn't want him to panic. It was late at night, so we decided to see how he did in the morning. During the night I came downstairs a few times to check on him. His breathing appeared to be less laboured, but he was sitting up. It was the worst night I've ever had.

The next morning H refused his food and milk. He came to sit under my chair, something he had done almost every morning for many years. Chris and I had our breakfast in silence with his laboured breathing in the background.

"He is suffering and we must not allow that to be prolonged. It would be unkind," Chris said.

I didn't need any persuasion. We called the surgery to arrange a time for a vet to come to the house. We wanted him to die in his own home. I did not want to let him go, but I had no option. It would be cruel to prolong his suffering. His cancer was terminal. I had never regarded Healey as an animal, but he had to die as one; to be put to sleep. He knew what was going on, this clever cat; he had tried to tell me last night when he asked for my lap. I got down and sat on the floor by him. He lifted his head to look at me. His eyes looked vacant. They were once so bright and pensive.

After breakfast Chris went upstairs to do some paper work. I sat on the kitchen floor close to Healey. I stroked him but he moved away from my hand, something he had never done before. Was he in great pain? I could only watch him. His fur had lost its shine. He sat there staring and not seeing, as though nothing would interest him anymore. He looked old and tired. I never thought about his age, all his twelve years and six months. He had been the same quiet, dependable and devoted friend year after year. I never thought he was mortal, like the rest of us. I had been fortunate to have had his love and company for so long. But is it not true that the more you have something good the more you want it to stay?

He got up. I watched as he walked purposely towards the backdoor, "I want to go out." Was he going out to meet death half way? He was looking up at the door handle. No, I could not let him out, he might find a quiet spot, lie down and die, alone and in pain. "Please don't go and die alone, I want to be by your side," I pleaded silently.

"Please, let me out." This time he looked at me. He must have seen my hesitation as he started to paw at the bottom of the door. I had opened this door to let him out a million times and every time he had come back. Would I trust him this time? Slowly I opened the door. He slipped out and disappeared round the corner. I left the door half shut and went to sit in front of the window.

I waited. Fifteen minutes (it felt like a life time) went by and I was getting very anxious. Then I saw him walking slowly down the garden path, stopping here and there to listen and sniff. I had stood here happily watching him do this walk a million times before. This time I had tears in my eyes. H was bidding farewell to his garden.

I heard the cat flap go in the porch. H walked in. Without a word he went to crouch under my chair. He had come back to me. I felt comforted that I didn't deprive him of his last walk. I offered him a saucer of warm milk, he didn't bother to sniff, he just turned his head away. It hurt me that he would not take comfort from me. Was he composing himself to die? Is that what cats do in their last hours, rejecting friends and loved ones? My presence had ceased to matter. H simply avoided looking me in the eye. He sat hunched looking at the carpet.

The vet came. It was Nicola, who had treated Healey many times and knew him well. She examined H and confirmed that the cancer had spread, and he had very little lung function left. She offered to give him a potent steroid injection to relieve the breathing.

"How long will that last?" I asked softly. I didn't want to alarm H.

"A couple of days," Nicola replied.

"A couple of days! And then what?"

There was a moment of silence so profound that I could hear my heart crying silently. I didn't want to burst into tears because I didn't want to cry with the vet and the nurse there. To prolong his life for a few days to ease my own pain was selfish mercy. Cats do not consciously decide to live or die, or whether they want a full burial or cremation. Healey had told me how he was doing last night. He told me again this morning, and because I loved him, I cared and I listened. Did I want to put him through surgery and treatment so that I could feel merciful?

I looked at Chris who was holding Healey in his lap. He didn't say a word. He had already made his diagnosis and decision hours ago. He knew what was best for the patient. I must make that decision myself. I looked at H, he was gazing ahead and far away. His face was a peculiar picture of remoteness and detachment, as if a burden had been lifted from his shoulders. He had done his work and it was time to move on. For a brief moment he turned to look at me as if to say, "we'll find each other again." H and I understood each other, we didn't need words. At that moment I knew: he was already reaching out for that rainbow, the one that he had promised me. I knew I must let him go, he would want me to do that.

"The steroid will be given for my benefit, not his. It is time I let him go," I whispered. I felt a prolonged silence in my heart as if it had stopped beating. The silence was interrupted only by the muffled sound of syringe and needle in the background. Nicola administered the injection that put H to sleep immediately. Healey died on Chris's lap, in my arms and in his beloved kitchen.

The vet and nurse left and Chris went to work promising he would come home as soon as he could to bury H.

"Don't hurry back," I told him. I needed time alone with H.

21. Two Farewells.

Healey was now lying peacefully on his side, in his basket in my studio. I went outside to pick a few daffodils from the garden, put them in a vase and placed it by the basket. There I sat with my friend. It may not be right to have a cat as your best friend, but what is right and what is wrong in this crazy world we live in, ruled and inhabited by human beings good and bad, kind and evil, saintly and twisted. I embrace my human race. Some of my friends and acquaintances are human beings. I also embraced as a best friend a small creature that came with four legs, a tail and a bagful of whiskers. H had come to me as an alien, and he had left as a friend.

We all know that death comes to us all one day, sooner or later, but the difference between living and non-living is so immense and final that it is still shocking to see that one minute someone is breathing and the next he is dead. In my years with H I had experienced the deaths of three women, who, in their own special way, had enriched my life; my mother, Chris's mother, and Ingrid's mother whom I called Mum. They all died of age-related natural causes. Ageing is the most merciless killer. It takes everyone away from you, and eventually it takes you away too.

I looked at my cat, his body was lifeless without his soul. Where was his soul now? I looked down at his face. His beautiful face looked peaceful and serene, in it I saw what he had always intended for me and what I had always believed in: his love for me. I bent to stroke his whiskers and eyes, they felt wet. Was he crying? Then I realised I was crying. I thought I was not going to cry. He was only a cat, but he was Healey. I let go and I wept and wept.

I talked to him about how we'd met, what he meant to me and how much I loved him. I told him that I realized we had met, and so we would part. I told him my life would go on normally without him for he was only a cat and he could be replaced!

Then I told myself I was lucky to have had Healey for so long. He had seen me through dark and bright days. He found me when I was feeling lost and helped anchor me to my new life in the country. The moment he crossed my threshold, the word home had a warm feel to it, he did all this without saying a word. This was not a cat that could be replaced.

I pulled gently at his whiskers and stroked his paws, and I held his left front paw firmly in both hands. I felt my heart stirred, a face appeared. It was my father's. What was he doing here! I was grieving for my cat, not for him.

****

I didn't hold my father's hand when he died. I had never held his hands. There was always something between me and his hands; his belt. He used it to beat me whenever he thought I had misbehaved. I had tried to reach out to him only once, in Queen Mary Hospital Hong Kong. My family rang to say that father had become very ill with diabetes and bladder cancer and he had a cardiac arrest in the emergency ward. Although he had recovered from the heart attack he might have only weeks to live.

I took leave from my work and flew back to Hong Kong. I wanted to see him when he was still alive. I had no idea why I wanted to do that. The distance between us and the passage of time had done nothing to ease the tension and strain between us. He resented the fact that I dared fly his nest. He had refused to sign the guardian's consent form when I needed it for my student visa to come to England. Mother consented. She signed it with the seal that bore her name.

I have vivid memory of that hospital visit. He appeared to be sleeping. The tough, invincible man that was my father wasn't there. Lying in the bed was a skeleton of a man, weak and dying. His eyes were firmly closed. I didn't think he was aware of my presence. Memories of his cruelty flooded back, I stiffened up. We never got to know each other. He had given me half of his genes, and we never found our common ground.

The cancer was eating him alive. I felt a sudden surge of emotion. Slowly and gently I moved closer to him. I looked at his thin and gnarled hands on the bed, I wanted to hold his hand. He stirred. I immediately withdrew my out stretched hand. He opened his eyes, they were like two main beams of a car, being turned full on in complete darkness. He stared at me. Was there a hint of acknowledgement ? I could not tell. Even when he was at his most vulnerable, there was still a hint of control, dominance and disregard in his gaze. I knew this look intimately. I opened my mouth to talk and no words came out. I began to feel ill at ease, his cold gaze was full of meaning. It was saying, "I have not changed my mind about you, I rather that you were not born to me. You are a great disappointment to me." I found it profoundly upsetting and fascinating at the same time. It was upsetting that my presence seemed to have unsettled him, fascinating that a father could bear grudges against his daughter for so long. What drove him? Where did this hatred and anger come from? What had I done? I felt an overwhelming emotion. Something moved me. I shed a tear and I immediately regretted it. He waved his hand for me to go. I didn't move. I looked into his eyes, held his gaze briefly and said, "Take care, father." He nodded. I walked out. It was the last time I saw my father. My memories of that visit have not diminished over the years.

With wisdom of hindsight and reflection, I don't think it is an exaggeration to say that I have got to know my father better in the years following his death than I ever did or could have done when he was alive. I have now a clear eyed portrait of my father as two men: one was charismatic, tough with a great sense of responsibility and drive, the other was stubborn, forceful, uncompromising and cruel.

Over the years I have learnt to understand the cause and effects of human relationship, now I believe my father didn't set out to crush me. He set his rules and expected everyone to live by them, and I didn't.

He died four months after my hospital visit. By his death bed were his two women and ten children. I did not return for the funeral, neither did my twin sister. I had bid my farewell.

****

After Healey's death, Joseph wandered in and sniffed at the body; he looked puzzled. I was puzzled too; at life's mystery. I started as an incurable cat phobic and here I was mourning the death of a great friend, my cat called H, a cat that found and lived out his destiny to the end; in his home, on this hillside and in my arms. H had realised his destiny when millions of us don't even know what our destinies are.

We buried him in one of his favourite spots. It is a sheltered patch between a bamboo and a white wisteria. We put him in the grave facing the kitchen window. I knew I'd never set eyes on H again but I also knew he would watch me from his final resting place.

It was a harrowing decision; putting a much loved cat to sleep. My head told me it was the right thing to do. My heart told me I should have given him, and myself, a second chance. Chris and I had made this decision with love, knowledge and careful consideration. I still had doubts afterwards: had we timed it right? What if …. ? I must admit it was a very painful decision, not a heroic act. I wasn't proud of myself.

H had achieved a heroic deed; he had made a huge effort to escape from the fate which surrounds domestic pets' lives. Dogs, cats, horses, chickens, pigs, cattle are all born to serve a function, to be in servitude to humans. They do their jobs, they breed, they die or they get slaughtered for food. H's four journeys back to his birthplace did not call for bravery and endurance alone, it demanded moral courage, he exercised will over fate. By pursuing his destiny I believe H had achieved an internal freedom; to pursue the life he wanted, and lived it out until he died. This level of achievement requires a break from upbringing and tradition, it requires a will of steel and an unwavering focus. The reward is much more than to securing the freedom to roam, like the wind, with no attachment, no root and no sense of purpose.

This great cat had walked his chosen path by my side. I had not influenced him, he had changed me. H was a class of his own. I was but his humble friend and fortunate companion.

H has returned to his roots. Only this time he will not return in body. Death has taken him away from me. But I know he is there for me; his body would become part of this hill, its earth and its water, they in turn would become the soul of his land; his beautiful and soulful eyes would become a star, the brightest of them all, it would shine upon this earth, and upon me in the darkest of nights; his soul would become part of the spring and autumn breezes, they would caress me when I walk upon our land, alone.

A living person is dead if he has no aspiration when alive;
A dead person is alive if he has fulfilled his aspirations when living.

22. A Cat Lives On.

True love stands the test of long separation.
As long as love endures,
The dream of reunion will come true.

(Anon)

It is now almost seven years since Healey passed away. I still look for him in my mind. I look in vain and I feel an ache in my heart.

His death has seemed so long ago that sometimes it feels it has happened in another life. At other times it feels it happened only moments ago and the memory is raw and painful. I have thought this can only apply to humans, but no!

He remains the recipient of many of my thoughts. How can he not, when I can feel his presence in every fabric of my immediate environment: my studio, the kitchen, the garden, the field, the canal, the river, the dual carriage-way with its roundabouts, which he crossed four times to get back to his land. Then there is the barn where he was born and the courtyard where it all began, all those years ago.

I have heard many stories about how small, furry angels discreetly entering people's lives out of the blue, only to perform great deeds, when done, they silently disappear.

It is still a mystery to me as to why this perfect creature should magically appear to grace my life, to offer me friendship and love at a time when I felt alone in a strange place. I still remember vividly how he would never make a noise, but would just sit there patiently, waiting for me to notice him. I still look to see whether he's there, on the garden wall, waiting to come in.

"OK, can you come out from hiding now, enough is enough! I miss you," I plead with him over his grave under the bamboo.

136

The bamboo sways in the gentle breeze, "I am here, I have never left your side," I hear him say. I know all the emotional turmoil is mine. I know cats, alive or dead, do not think and feel the way I do.

****

I remember aspects of life with H with so much fondness and pleasure I want to dwell on them. Allowing myself to be adopted by a stubborn cat turned out to be such great fun; and when this cat turned out to be a sage in disguise, the experience was simply life changing. H is worthy to be an immortal.

The magic with Healey was the timing. Fate put him there at a time when I needed a distraction, something for me to fight against; something to divert me from the destructive force of an isolated life. It had probably saved my marriage too; I was so busy fighting this cat that I had neither the time nor the energy to indulge in self pity. My love for a cat has been a great surprise to families and friends. They all know my history of cat phobia. Well, it has surprised me too.

H embraced me in his big heart and helped me overcome my fear of cats. He has taught me a lot about cats: their individuality, idiosyncrasy and above all their capacity for love and friendship, which they do not give away thoughtlessly. Cats understand life in its simplest form: no fuss, no ambition, no worries and no imagined fears. They are their own masters who seek solitude and freedom. If they choose to allow you into their world, consider yourself fortunate.

A Chinese proverb says: *If you want something, give it first.* H has shown me how to do it with cats: be the first one to show friendship, to offer love and affection. They know and they would reward you with their purring songs and soulful looks.

I have since met and befriended many cats. I recognise their signals and know how to respond. When I see a cat, tail up in the air, come towards me with it held high and straight, I recognise this is a sign of friendship mixed with confidence. Now I understand this gesture I see it everywhere. I tell them they are beautiful, I stroke them, play with them when they are playful, leave them to themselves when they prefer to be alone. I have learnt never to force a cat into something contrary to their mood. My cat loving friends are right all along: Cats are God's best gift. Big H is one of the very best and he IS mine. If I had to live over all those years again I wouldn't change a thing. OK, I might have consulted a couple of cat websites more carefully. With the knowledge and experience I have now I might one day consider setting up a victim support group for incurable cat phobics.

****

Joseph is now head of the family, a role he fulfils with gusto and dedication. He follows me around everywhere, just like Healey used to do. He's taken over the job of saying hello, which he always left to H before. He still retains some of his alpha male kitten- like way, but he has grown into a trusting and contented cat. He knows he is loved and spoiled and he indulges in our affection.

"It is wet out there! I want my f—o—o—d." JJ has just walked into my studio. He hurls his big body on the ground in front of me, flopping down, stretching and reaching out with his paws, he wants his f—o—o—d.

It has been raining heavily the whole morning. I look out of the window. The rain has just stopped. A huge rainbow stretches right across the valley down below. A few birds are flying nearby.

Do I see the silhouette of a cat at the very top of the rainbow? Yes, I can see him clearly: the soulful eyes and the three winged butterfly. H is not dead, he has just merely gone before me to a world of rainbow, a paradise for cats and their friends. After all how can a paradise be a paradise without one's good friend. H is waiting patiently, he knows: I won't hurry. When the time comes, my cat and I will sit together on the rainbow, and watch the clouds go by.

Life has an end,
Love has no end.

(Anon)

**********The End**********